Donald Margulies

Set design by Neil Patel   *Photos by Joan Marcus*
Lisa Emery and Julie White (top), and Kevin Kilner and Matthew Arkin in
the New York production of *Dinner with Friends* at the Variety Arts Theatre.

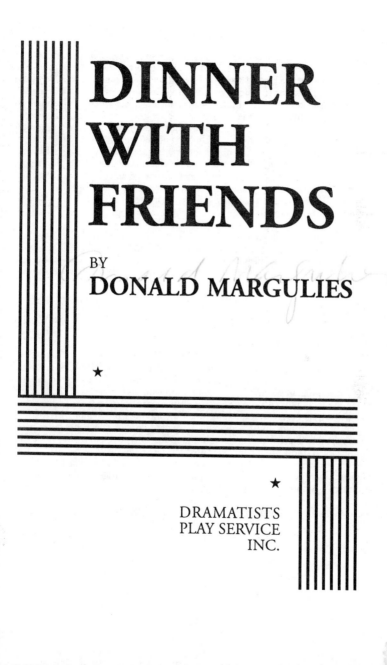

DINNER
WITH
FRIENDS

BY
DONALD MARGULIES

★

★

DRAMATISTS
PLAY SERVICE
INC.

DINNER WITH FRIENDS
Copyright © 2000, Donald Margulies

All Rights Reserved

Commissioned by and premiered at ACTORS THEATRE OF LOUISVILLE

Subsequently produced by South Coast Repertory

Originally produced Off-Broadway by:

| Mitchell Maxwell | Mark Balsam | Ted Tulchin |
| Victoria Maxwell | Mari Nakachi | Steven Tulchin |

for Lynn

DINNER WITH FRIENDS was commissioned by Actors Theatre of Louisville (Jon Jory, Producing Director) and had its world premiere at the Humana Festival of New American Plays in March 1998. It was directed by Michael Bloom; the set design was by Paul Owen; the lighting design was by Greg Sullivan; the sound design was by Michael Rasbury; the costume design was by Jeanette deJong; and the stage manager was Becky Owczarski. The cast was as follows:

GABE .... Adam Grupper
KAREN .... Linda Purl
BETH .... Devora Millman
TOM .... David Byron

A revised version of DINNER WITH FRIENDS was presented by South Coast Repertory (David Emmes, Producing Artistic Director; Martin Benson, Artistic Director) in Costa Mesa, California, in October 1998. It was directed by Daniel Sullivan; the set design was by Thomas Lynch; the lighting design was by Pat Collins; the music and sound design were by Michael Roth; the costume design was by Candice Cain; and the production stage manager was Scott Hamilton. The cast was as follows:

GABE .... John Carroll Lynch
KAREN .... Jane Kaczmarek
BETH .... Julie White
TOM .... T. Scott Cunningham

DINNER WITH FRIENDS was further revised and presented by Mitchell Maxwell, Mark Balsam, Victoria Maxwell, Ted Tulchin, Mari Nakachi, and Steven Tulchin at the Stamford (Connecticut) Center for the Arts (George E. Moredock III, Executive Director) in October 1999. The play had its New York City premiere at the Variety Arts Theatre on November 4, 1999. It was directed by Daniel Sullivan; the set design was by Neil Patel; the lighting design was by Rui Rita; the sound design was by Peter Fitzgerald; the original music was by Michael Roth; the costume design was by Jess Goldstein; the production stage manager was R. Wade Jackson; and the assistant stage manager was Deirdre McCrane. The cast was as follows:

GABE .... Matthew Arkin
KAREN .... Lisa Emery
BETH .... Julie White*
TOM .... Kevin Kilner

* Carolyn McCormick replaced Julie White in January 2000.

CHARACTERS

KAREN and GABE
and
TOM and BETH,
two couples in their forties.

PLACE

ACT ONE

Scene 1: Karen and Gabe's kitchen in Connecticut.
Evening. Winter.

Scene 2: Tom and Beth's bedroom.
Later that night.

Scene 3: Karen and Gabe's living room.
Later still.

ACT TWO

Scene 1: A house in Martha's Vineyard.
Summer. Twelve and a half years earlier.

Scene 2: Karen and Gabe's patio.
Spring. A few months after the events in Act One.

Scene 3: A bar in Manhattan.
Later that afternoon.

Scene 4: Karen and Gabe's bedroom. Martha's Vineyard.
That night.

DINNER WITH FRIENDS

ACT ONE

Scene 1

Gabe and Karen's eat-in kitchen. A snowy night in suburban New England. The present. Gabe and Karen are entertaining their good friend Beth at an informal dinner, which is now moving on to the dessert course. Dishes are being cleared; coffee is being prepared. Four children, now offstage, had been seated at the table with them. Beth is distracted but not impolite.

GABE. Oh, and this *market* she took us to!
KAREN. She took us shopping.
BETH. Uh huh.
GABE. *Campo di Fiori.*
KAREN. This indoor market.
GABE. Fish, produce, you name it!
KAREN. Gorgeous stuff. Really.
GABE. Rabbits, goats …
KAREN. So aromatic. So … colorful. And the faces!
GABE. I got some great shots.
KAREN. The *authority* with which she handled every onion, every red pepper!
BETH. Huh.
GABE. She'd squeeze an eggplant just so, and close her eyes and inhale … *(He demonstrates. Beth smiles.)*
KAREN. This is someone who's been cooking for seventy-five years. Can you imagine?

7

BETH. Wow.

GABE. Her relationship to food is so primal, so *sexy*, really. Gave us a great angle for our piece.

BETH. Huh!

KAREN. *(Over "Huh!")* Well, I don't know about *sexy* ... She's eighty-six years old.

GABE. Yeah, but you see the way she handles a zucchini?

KAREN. *(To Beth.)* Regular or decaf?

BETH. Uh ... *(Looks at the clock.)* Better make it decaf. *(She gathers a few plates; Gabe takes them from her.)* Let me do something.

GABE. *(Sotto.)* No, no, sit. *(Beth does, reluctantly.)*

KAREN. The *traffic* to her place was absolutely horrific.

BETH. Oh, really?

GABE. Harrowing. Truly.

KAREN. What are *you* complaining about? *I* did the driving.

GABE. I know. *(To Beth.)* She's amazing: She drives like a New York cabbie; she *does*. I couldn't drive; I was too culture-shocked. I was afraid I'd get us killed. Our bodies'd have to be shipped home through the State Department ...

BETH. Uch! Gabe!

GABE. ... You and Tom would become the boys' guardians, raise them on processed foods ... *(She swipes at him affectionately for his affectionate dig.)*

KAREN. Is that really what was going through your head?

GABE. Absolutely.

KAREN. You are one morbid dude, my darling.

GABE. Yes, and I'm all yours. *(They kiss.)*

BETH. So did you ever get to Rome?

GABE. *(Confused by her question.)* What?

KAREN. This *is* Rome, Beth.

GABE. Emilia lives outside of Rome.

KAREN. Remember?

BETH. *(Over " ... Rome.")* Oh, of course, I'm sorry, I thought this was *Florence* you were talking about.

GABE. *(Over " ... you were talking about.")* No no, we haven't gotten to Florence yet.

KAREN. Is this really boring?

BETH. No no, not at all.

KAREN. It is, we'll shut up.

BETH. No no, go on. I want to hear about it. I do.

KAREN. Why don't we just get to lunch.

GABE. Okay, so we get there in one piece ...

BETH. Yeah...?

GABE. I am *drenched* with sweat from the hellish journey, I stumble out of the car, feeling a bit queasy ...

KAREN. And she's preparing this *lunch*...!

GABE. This feast!

BETH. Wow.

KAREN. The simplest, freshest ...

GABE. Uh! The *pomodoro!* Tell her about the *pomodoro!*

KAREN. Right. She had this lovely sunny little pantry ...

BETH. Yeah...?

GABE. *Filled* with jars and jars ...

KAREN. Jars and jars of her own plum tomatoes picked from her own garden that were the most incredible, succulent ...

GABE. You wouldn't believe how *red* these tomatoes were ...

BETH. Hm ...

GABE. ... and sweet!

KAREN. They were so *soft,* Beth ...

GABE. Buttery, almost.

KAREN. They *were.* And she just *crushed* them with her bare hands.

BETH. Huh!

GABE. *Pul*verized them ...

KAREN. You should've seen ...

GABE. ... in her gnarled little hands. It was a riot, this little old lady ...

KAREN. It was funny, it really was.

BETH. *(Smiling.)* Uh huh.

GABE. I mean, she's really *tiny,* like four-ten or something.

KAREN. No ...

GABE. She's got to be, honey; come on, she's definitely under five feet.

KAREN. No, she's not, not *under* ...

GABE. *(Over " ... under ... ")* Think about it, she was like up to

9

here on me.

KAREN. No she wasn't.

GABE. Yes she was, don't you remember how she — ?

BETH. *Any*way.

GABE. Anyway, the *pomodoro*.

KAREN. The *pomodoro* was amazing.

GABE. And simple.

KAREN. Amazingly simple. Sauteed garlic …

BETH. Yeah…?

GABE. A *lot* of garlic.

KAREN. A little onion. Finely diced.

GABE. That's right. That was interesting: Very little onion.

KAREN. Are you gonna let me tell this, or what?

GABE. Sorry.

KAREN. She crushes the garlic with her *thumb,* by the way. This arthritic, calcified thumb. It was hilarious.

GABE. *(Over " … hilarious.")* Mashes it into the marble counter, *flings* it into the olive oil.

KAREN. Then the tomatoes.

GABE. Five, six pounds of them.

BETH. Huh!

KAREN. Breaks up whatever isn't crushed with the wooden spoon.

GABE. Right. Very deliberately, while stirring, flames shooting, scalding sauce sputtering everywhere.

KAREN. No no, she used a screen.

GABE. You sure?

KAREN. Positive. Then she adds a fistful of parsley …

BETH. Uh huh.

KAREN. Handful of sugar, handful of salt. Lots of fresh ground pepper.

BOY'S VOICE. *(From upstairs.)* DAD!

KAREN. Throws in some chianti.

GABE. Which she'd been discreetly tucking away the whole time.

BOY'S VOICE. DADDY?!!

GABE. *(Calls.)* YES?

CHILDREN'S VOICES. PUT ON A TAPE! WE WANT TO WATCH A TAPE! PLEEEASSE?!

10

GABE. *(Shouts back.)* DANNY CAN DO IT!

BOY'S VOICE. NO, DAD! I CAN'T! *YOU* DO IT!

GABE. *(Over "You do it!")* YES, YOU CAN; DANNY, YOU DO IT ALL THE TIME. ALL YOU DO IS PUT IT IN AND PRESS PLAY …

BOY'S VOICE. I *CAN'T* DO IT! I WANT *YOU* TO DO IT!

KAREN. *(Over "I want you to do it!" To Gabe.)* Will you just go do it?

GABE. He can do it, he knows how to do it.

BOY'S VOICE. *(Over " … he knows how to do it.")* DAD! WE WANT TO WATCH *THE ARISTOCATS*! IT ISN'T WORKING!

GABE. *(Shouts.)* MAKE SURE THE TV IS ON CHANNEL THREE!

BOY'S VOICE. WHAT?

GABE. CHANNEL THREE!

KAREN. Please, Gabe. I hate when you shout back and forth like that. Just go up there and talk to them.

GABE. *(Calls.)* All right, I'LL BE RIGHT UP! *(Starts to go.)* Don't talk about Florence without me. *(He goes. Pause. Karen smiles uncomfortably, sensing something is wrong.)*

KAREN. So … *(A beat.)* Is everything…? Was dinner…?

BETH. No, no, dinner was great. The lamb and risotto, everything was fabulous.

KAREN. I overcooked the risotto; it was a bit gummy.

BETH. Not at all. It was perfect.

KAREN. We've been running off at the mouth all night; I'm sorry.

BETH. No, no, you're excited. I'm jealous; it sounds like a great trip.

KAREN. It was. It was really good for us. We were so trepidatious about leaving the boys …

BETH. I'm sure.

KAREN. Ten days is a long time.

BETH. It is.

KAREN. We missed them terribly. We talked about them all the time, of course …

BETH. Of course.

KAREN. But they were fine. They totally wore my *mother* out, but they ... *Next* time you and Tom have got to come with us.

BETH. Uh huh.

KAREN. We'd have a blast, don't you think?

BETH. Oh, yeah.

KAREN. Just the four of us?! You would *love* Italy. The art...!

BETH. I know; I can't believe I've never been there.

KAREN. Leave the kids with Tom's sister or something. They'll survive. Believe me, with Danny and Isaac, we came home and it was like, "Oh, hello; *you* again?" *(They smile. Silence.)* Too bad about Tommy.

BETH. What do you mean?

KAREN. Having to fly to Washington on a night like this.

BETH. Oh, yeah.

KAREN. *His* loss. Oh, well, more food for us. *(They smile. A beat.)* Are you okay?

BETH. Oh, yeah; I think I may have a migraine coming on, that's all.

KAREN. Oh! *(That explains Beth's behavior.)* Well, lay off the wine.

BETH. I am; I have been.

KAREN. You want some Motrin?

BETH. Yeah, good idea, thanks. *(Karen gets pills from a cabinet.)*

KAREN. I almost forgot: We got you guys something.

BETH. Oh, really? How nice.

KAREN. Just a little something. For the house. *You* know. *(Karen gives Beth a wrapped bundle.)*

BETH. Thanks. Should I open it now?

KAREN. Whatever. *(Beth unwraps the bundle: place mats. They somehow sadden her, but she tries not to let it show.)*

BETH. Oh, Karen, thank you so much.

KAREN. They're place mats.

BETH. Yes. They're beautiful.

KAREN. From Siena. We spent a day there. Can you use them?

BETH. Oh, God, yes, *me*? *(Gabe returns holding four bowls, which had been the kids' ice cream dessert.)*

GABE. You should see: I wish I had some film.

KAREN. That's right: We ran out of film.

GABE. *(Continuous.)* All four kids, all in a row, like this, *(Head in hands.)* like four little Raphael cherubs, watching *The Aristocats*

for the ninety-seventh time. *(Beth suddenly breaks down and sobs.)*
KAREN. Beth?
GABE. *(Over "Beth?")* What is it? What's the matter? *(Beth sobs piteously.)*
KAREN. Oh, my God …
GABE. *(Softly, to Karen.)* Did I miss something here?
KAREN. *(Shrugs, then:)* Beth, what is it?
BETH. Oh, Karen … Tom's leaving me.
KAREN. What?
BETH. He's leaving me.
GABE. What are you talking about?
BETH. He doesn't love me anymore. He's leaving. He left me. He's gone. *(She breaks down again.)*
GABE. What happened?
BETH. He says he's in love with someone else.
KAREN. Oh, God, you're kidding! *(Beth shakes her head.)*
GABE. Who?
KAREN. *(Admonishing.)* Gabe!
GABE. What, I want to know if it's someone we know!
KAREN. What difference does it make?
BETH. It's okay. I don't know, some stewardess.
GABE. A *stew*ardess? Tom's in love with a *stew*ardess?
KAREN. Oh, God, that is so tacky.
BETH. He's been traveling so much … "Nancy" her name is.
KAREN. How long has this been going on?
BETH. I don't know, a few months, apparently.
KAREN. *(Over " … apparently.")* A few *months?* When did you find out?
BETH. Last week; while you were away.
GABE. *(Softly.)* Oh, jeez …
KAREN. What happened?
BETH. He confessed. We had an argument. About the dog. He hates the dog. If the dog chews on the rug, naturally it's *my* fault, so … *(Takes a breath.)* He told me he was miserable, that he's always been miserable …
GABE. What?
BETH. *(Continuous.)* … he's been miserable for so long he doesn't remember what it was like to be happy.

13

GABE. *Tom* said that?

BETH. *(Nods, then:)* He said this isn't the life he had in mind for himself, that if he were to stay married to me, it would kill him, he would die young.

GABE. Jesus.

BETH. *(To Gabe.)* Did you know about this? Did he say anything to you?

GABE. *(Over " … to you?")* No! This is totally … I didn't have a *clue* …

KAREN. We all just went out to eat together.

BETH. I know.

KAREN. Right before we left. That Indian place in Branford. We loved their chicken *tikka masala*.

BETH. I know; that's right.

KAREN. You seemed fine; both of you did. He didn't seem "miserable" at all.

BETH. I know.

KAREN. You mean to tell me we were sitting there having a wonderful time and he was not only miserable but in love with someone else?!

BETH. I know, isn't that…?

KAREN. Oh, sweetie, I'm so sorry, this can't be happening … How could he do this to you? I just can't believe it. *(To Gabe, off his silence.)* Feel free; jump in any time.

GABE. *(Defensively.)* What. *(She gives him a look.)* I'm listening.

KAREN. *(To Beth.)* So, are you getting some counseling or something?

BETH. *(Shakes her head, then:)* He doesn't want to.

KAREN. Come on! Twelve years, two kids: He doesn't *want* to?

GABE. What *does* he want? A trial separation or something?

BETH. No, no, he wants a divorce.

GABE. A divorce?!

KAREN. Oh, that's ridiculous.

BETH. That's what he *says* … He says he's tried for years to work it out …

KAREN. *How? How* did he try?

BETH. *(Continuous.)* He's had it, he's spent, he can't give it anymore.

14

GABE. I don't get it; this just doesn't sound like Tom. It's like his body's been snatched and he's been replaced by a pod.

BETH. I know. You should have seen him. The rage! I didn't recognize him. I've never seen that kind of rage in him before! He *hates* me.

KAREN. *(Soothing.)* No …

BETH. He does. He says I've ruined his life.

KAREN. Well, this sounds like something else is going on.

BETH. Doesn't it?

KAREN. Some kind of life-crisis thing. God, I wish you guys had come with us to Italy!

BETH. I think he's really in trouble. I tried telling him that, but that only made him angrier.

KAREN. Oh, this is classic. We've got to get him some help.

BETH. Good luck. You know Tom: He's suspicious of every kind of therapy you can think of. I'm just worried he's headed for some kind of breakdown.

KAREN. Do you think it's drugs?

GABE. Karen …

KAREN. How else do you account for something like this? It's a total personality transformation.

BETH. Karen, I've been racking my brain, playing back every little tiff, every long-distance phone conversation …

KAREN. He's crazy about you, Beth! I know it! I've seen it! You can't fake something like that.

BETH. *(Over " … something like that.")* Karen. The things he said to me … This is not a man who's crazy about me, believe me. He's in love with this person. He *is*. He says she's everything I'm not.

KAREN. What is that supposed to mean?

BETH. He says she's completely devoted to him. She hangs on his every word. She's "there" for him.

KAREN. Oh, God, such bullshit.

BETH. Really. The stuff pouring out of his mouth … It's like bad greeting cards. He says *I* gave him seventy-five percent, *she* gives him a hundred and twenty.

KAREN. He said that? A hundred and twenty percent? *(Beth nods.)* He's into percentages? What's that extra twenty percent supposed to be? *(Beth and Gabe look at her.)*

15

GABE. Karen.

KAREN. Oh. *(To Beth.)* What, you didn't go for that extra twenty percent?

BETH. Apparently not like *she* does. *(Pause.)*

KAREN. Look, we'll *talk* to him. *Gabe* will.

GABE. Sure, I'll ...

BETH. *(Over "Sure, I'll ... ")* No, Karen, he wants out. There's nothing to talk about. I *told* him: Whatever it would take; I would do *any*thing.

KAREN. Did you know he was so miserable?

BETH. No! He says I ignored all the signs, I didn't "hear" him ... I mean, if only he'd *talked* to me, really *talked* to me. He was moody. Yes. Distracted. I thought it was work. Or jet lag ... I'd find him staring off into space and ask him what he was thinking and he'd always say, Nothing. *(Karen looks at Gabe; that sounds familiar.)*

GABE. *(Defensively.)* What. *(Karen shakes her head.)*

BETH. I don't know, he's definitely been going *through* something, that much I know.

KAREN. Like what?

BETH. Oh, I don't know that I want to go into it.

KAREN. That's okay.

BETH. Inappropriate stuff. You know: sexual stuff. *(A breath.)* We went out to the movies. Some stupid *action* thing he wanted to see, nothing sexy, and Tom like puts my hand in his crotch to *you* know, and I look at him like, What are you crazy? And he's mortally offended!

KAREN. Was this before or after the girlfriend?

BETH. Must've been after.

KAREN. Uh huh, uh huh.

BETH. Some kind of sexual-daring test and I flunked it.

KAREN. That's right, one more nail in the old coffin.

BETH. You got it.

GABE. See that? One lousy hand job, you could've saved your marriage.

KAREN. Gabe!

GABE. Sorry.

KAREN. So, is she the reason he flew to Washington? *(Beth nods.)*

16

BOY'S VOICE. DAD!! FIX THE TAPE!

KAREN. Oh, God, what about the kids? Have you told them? *(Beth shakes her head sadly.)*

CHILDREN'S VOICES. *(Variously.)* FIX IT! FIX THE TAPE!! *(Etc.)*

KAREN. *(Shouts upstairs.)* WE HEAR YOU! STOP SHOUTING! *(To Beth.)* When are you going to?

BETH. I don't know. He goes out of town so much, I feel like there's no need to break it to them right away, you know? Maybe we're a bit more testy than usual but things really aren't that different.

BOY'S VOICE. DAD! IT'S DOING THAT *THING* AGAIN!

GABE. *(Shouts.)* YOU CAN FIX IT, DANNY!

BOY'S VOICE. I DON'T KNOW HOW!

GABE. I SHOWED YOU! REMEMBER?!

KAREN. *(Shouts, over "Remember?!")* DADDY SHOWED YOU, DANIEL!

GABE. *(Shouts, over " … Daniel!")* THE PLUS AND THE MINUS! PRESS THEM BOTH AT THE SAME TIME!

KAREN. Gabe. *Must* you?

GABE. I'll go up …

KAREN. No no, I will.

CHILDREN'S VOICES. FIX IT! IT'S STILL DOING IT!

KAREN. I'M *COMING!* STOP *SHOUTING!* *(She goes. Gabe and Beth are alone. Awkward silence. He offers her wine; Beth shakes her head; Gabe refills his own glass. Pause.)*

GABE. All the vacations we spent on the Vineyard … *(A beat.)* You guys *met* there; we had such great *times* there. *(A beat.)* Remember the summer you and Karen were both pregnant? *(Beth nods. They ruminate bittersweetly in silence. Gabe sighs, shakes his head incredulously, sips his wine.)*

CHILDREN'S VOICES. YAYY!!!

GABE. How can he walk away? I don't understand it. How can he just…?

BETH. *(Gets up, distracted.)* I should get the kids; we should get going. *(She picks up one boy's sneaker by its laces, looks around for the other.)* Do you see another one of these? *(Gabe takes her hand in a loving, friendly way.)*

GABE. Beth … *(She stops, looks at him.)* I'm so sorry.

17

BETH. You thought Tom never should've married me.

GABE. What?

BETH. It's okay, Gabe; I know; Tom told me.

GABE. I never said that.

BETH. It's okay. I just wonder if you were right. *(Karen returns, notes a certain tension, embraces Beth.)*

KAREN. Why don't we have dessert?

BETH. Oh, I don't know, it's late; I really should get them home.

KAREN. Don't. They're riveted.

BETH. You're right, what am I running home to? *(She sits.)*

KAREN. *(To Gabe; re: dessert.)* You want to do the honors?

GABE. Sure.

BETH. I'm sorry to lay this on you guys ...

GABE. *(Dismissively.)* Hey ...

KAREN. *(Over "Hey ... ")* Don't be silly ...

BETH. This is the last thing you were expecting tonight, huh?

GABE. Oh, God, yes. *(He brings a cake to the table, slices it; Karen refills coffee, etc.)*

BETH. Oh, that looks so good, what is it?

GABE. *Limone-mandorle-polenta.*

BETH. *Mandorle?*

GABE. Almond.

BETH. Mm.

KAREN. Instead of white flour, you use polenta.

BETH. Ooo, what a good idea.

GABE. And *six* eggs.

KAREN. It's very eggy.

GABE. And a *ton* of butter.

BETH. *(Tastes it.)* Mm, it's delicious.

KAREN. *(Samples it; approvingly.)* Hm.

GABE. I think it's great.

KAREN. Yeah? You don't think I could've beaten the eggs a little bit longer? Don't you think it could've been a little fluffier?

GABE. No. I think it's good.

BETH. It's wonderful.

KAREN. *(To Gabe.)* Too much vanilla?

GABE. *(Considers this.)* Uh ... possibly.

KAREN. *(Concurs.)* Hm. *(Silence while they eat.)*

18

BETH. *(Sighs.)* I feel so much better now that I told you. All night long, sitting here, I thought I was gonna burst. You're my closest friends, you know.

KAREN. Of course we are.

GABE. Of course.

BETH. My closest friends in the world. *(They eat in silence.)* Mm, this is so good! *(Karen and Gabe are pensive.)*

Scene 2

Later that night. Beth and Tom's cluttered, messy bedroom in lamp light. Piles of books, magazines and clothes are about. Beth, seeming vulnerable and bereft in her own home, disrobes and, wearing a T-shirt and panties, gets into bed. Somewhere in the house, a dog barks.

BETH. Sarge! *(Pause. More barking.)* Sarge! Quiet! *(Pause. The barking persists.)* Sergeant, dammit, be quiet! *(The bedroom door opens, startling her; she gasps. Tom, in from the cold, dressed in winter gear, tracking snow in on his boots, stands there. Light from the hallway spills in.)* Tom! Jesus ...

TOM. *(Overlap; whispers.)* Sorry. I didn't mean to ...

BETH. *(Overlap; normal volume.)* Couldn't you at least knock?

TOM. I'm sorry.

BETH. You can't just come and go as you please anymore, Tom ...

TOM. Shhh ...

BETH. *(Continuous.)* ... it's not fair; if you're gonna go, go.

TOM. I just wanted to ...

BETH. *(Continuous.)* Otherwise, I'm gonna have to change the locks.

TOM. Come on, you don't want to do *that* ...

BETH. I *am,* that's what I'm gonna have to do.

TOM. *(Over " ... have to do.")* Look, I didn't come here to fight. Okay? I saw the light on; I just wanted to say hi.

19

BETH. "Hi"?! Why aren't you in D.C.?

TOM. My flight was cancelled; they closed the airport.

BETH. Why, the snow's not that bad.

TOM. No, but it is getting worse. See? It's really starting to come down.

BETH. *(Glances out.)* Oh, shit, it is. Why didn't you get a room at the airport?

TOM. There *were* no rooms at the airport; you mean a motel?

BETH. Yeah.

TOM. There were no *rooms,* nothing, everything was booked.

BETH. Everything?

TOM. There was not a room to be had. I swear. You should've seen what was going on there. Everybody shouting and pushing … I just didn't have it in me to stay and sleep on the floor.

BETH. Why didn't you call your friend, the stewardess?

TOM. *(Wearily.)* Travel agent.

BETH. Whatever.

TOM. I did.

BETH. And? Couldn't *she* help you? With all her many connections?

TOM. Not really; no. I was forty-five minutes from home. All I could think about … was coming home. *(They share eye contact. Off her look:)* Don't worry, I'm sleeping in the den.

BETH. Who's worried?

TOM. Well, look, I just wanted to say hi.

BETH. You're melting.

TOM. Huh?

BETH. Your boots. You're making a puddle.

TOM. Oh. Sorry … *(He sits to remove his boots.)* I looked in on the kids; they both look pretty wrecked.

BETH. Oh, yeah, they partied hearty. Sam fell asleep in the car. I made a successful transfer, though; he didn't budge.

TOM. He's snoring his head off in there.

BETH. He's getting a cold.

TOM. *(Sympathetically.)* Oh no …

BETH. His nose was runny all night. I gave him some Tylenol before we left Karen and Gabe's.

TOM. Liquid or chewable?

BETH. Liquid.

TOM. Wow. And he let you? He usually puts up such a fight. Remember how he'd make himself gag?

BETH. *(Discomfited by the familiarity of their conversation, she changes the subject.)* Yeah, well, look, I'd really like to be alone right now if you don't mind ...

TOM. *(Over "... if you don't mind ... ")* Yeah, sure ...

BETH. Your bedding's in the dryer.

TOM. Oh. Thanks.

BETH. I threw everything in the wash. I wasn't expecting you back.

TOM. I know. Thank you. I'll ...

BETH. You might want to grab an extra blanket while you're at it; sounds like it might get pretty cold in there tonight.

TOM. Good idea, thanks. *(Gets blanket from a chest. Sees the place mats.)* What's this?

BETH. Oh. For us. From Italy. A little house gift. Very homey, no? Karen and Gabe, God love 'em, they know what a disaster I am in the kitchen so they're always giving me things like trivets and cookbooks.

TOM. *(Smiles, then:)* How was dinner?

BETH. Fabulous. *You* know. When is dinner there *not* fabulous?

TOM. What was it this time?

BETH. Oh, *you* know. These incredible recipes they picked up in Italy. Pumpkin risotto, grilled lamb ...

TOM. Mm. That *does* sound good. You didn't bring any home by any chance?

BETH. No; I did not.

TOM. The kids eat that, too?

BETH. Of course not, what do you think? They would never eat anything that good. No, Gabe cooked up some macaroni and cheese for them. From scratch. That was almost as good as the risotto.

TOM. *(A beat.)* So how are they?

BETH. They're fine. *You* know. As always. They went on and on about Italy. Thank God their slides weren't back yet.

TOM. *(Smiles, then:)* So what did you tell them?

BETH. About what?

TOM. Why I wasn't there.

BETH. I said you had to go to D.C.

TOM. And they accepted that?

BETH. Why shouldn't they accept that? You're always going *some* where …

TOM. Yeah, but they didn't suspect anything?

BETH. No.

TOM. What did they say?

BETH. What do you mean, what did they say? What did they say about what?

TOM. About my not being there.

BETH. They said they were sorry.

TOM. Sorry about what?

BETH. About your not being there! Jesus! Are you gonna cross-*examine* me now? Look, I'm tired, I'm going to sleep …

TOM. I just want to get an idea of what you all talked about, that's all.

BETH. I told you. Italy and stuff. They talked about this famous old Italian cook they're doing a piece on.

TOM. And?

BETH. I don't know, Tom, we talked about a lot of things; what do we ever talk about?

TOM. I don't know, what *do* we talk about?

BETH. Movies, kids, money, the news, I don't know, what we saw, what we read. Karen's mom has cataracts; she has to have surgery.

TOM. Is that it?

BETH. I don't know, I don't remember every single goddamn thing.

TOM. You were there like five or six hours.

BETH. Oh, please …

TOM. Right? Like from five to ten, ten-thirty?

BETH. So?

TOM. That's a lot of hours to fill with talk. You mean to tell me the whole evening went by without a word about us?

BETH. You are so paranoid, you know that?

TOM. Oh, really, am I?

BETH. *(Gets under the covers, turns away.)* Look, I'm really not in the mood for this …

TOM. You told them.

BETH. What?!

22

TOM. You did! You told them!

BETH. Oh, God …

TOM. I can tell by looking at you! I *knew* I shouldn't've trusted you!

BETH. Shhh! You want to wake up the whole house?!

TOM. *(Continuous.)* We were gonna get a sitter and tell them together, face to face, remember?! That's all I asked: Wait for me to get back, we'll tell them together.

BETH. *(Over " … we'll tell them together.")* If it was really so important to you, you should've just come tonight, instead of running off to be with your girlfriend!

TOM. Shit, where were the kids?

BETH. What?

TOM. Where were the kids when you told them?

BETH. I don't know …

TOM. You don't *know?!* Were they *sitting* there?!

BETH. No, of course not. They were upstairs, I guess, watching a tape.

TOM. What were they watching?

BETH. What?!

TOM. What tape were they watching?

BETH. Christ, I don't know, Tom …

TOM. You don't know what tape your own children were watching?!

BETH. Oh, for God's sake … I don't know, some Disney thing. *The Aristocats.*

TOM. *(Pacing, agitated.)* So, the kids are upstairs watching *The Aristocats* and you're where?

BETH. This is ridiculous.

TOM. No no, I want to get the whole picture. The kids are upstairs and you're in the living room? Huh?

BETH. *(Reluctantly.)* At the table.

TOM. Middle of dinner?

BETH. Right before dessert.

TOM. What was it?

BETH. What.

TOM. The dessert.

BETH. Some kind of lemon-almond cake, made with polenta.

TOM. Was it great?

BETH. Yes.

TOM. So you're sitting there …

BETH. I don't believe this.

TOM. Tell me.

BETH. We were sitting there … and I lost it. I just … lost it.

TOM. Oh, Christ … You *cried?* You actually *cried?*

BETH. Yes. What do you expect? Of course I cried.

TOM. Shit!

BETH. *You* try carrying that around with you. I'm only human. I mean, I'm sitting there with our closest friends …

TOM. I can't believe you did this …

BETH. *(Continuous.)* … eating their food, drinking their wine, making believe that everything is just dandy, and I couldn't do it!

TOM. I can't believe it …

BETH. So what? So what if they know? So they know! They were bound to find out!

TOM. That's not the point! *You've* got the advantage now!

BETH. What?! I do not!

TOM. Of course you do! You got to them first!

BETH. Tom …

TOM. *(Continuous.)* They heard your side of the story first! Of *course* they're gonna side with you, it's only natural!

BETH. Oh, come on, nobody's taking sides.

TOM. Don't be naive! You know how it is! I'm not gonna let you get away with this …

BETH. What?!

TOM. *(Continuous.)* Gabe and Karen mean too much to me, I'm not gonna let you turn them against me!

BETH. Tom, you're overreacting.

TOM. Don't tell me I'm overreacting! You've prejudiced my case!

BETH. I have not, Tommy. I was very evenhanded.

TOM. How can you say that?! You're sitting there turning on the tears …

BETH. I wasn't turning on anything! Fuck you; I stated the facts. They were very sympathetic.

TOM. Of course they were sympathetic. You won them over.

BETH. I did not; stop saying that.

TOM. You *intended* to tell them.

BETH. That is not true! I tried, I really did. I couldn't help it!

Everything just spilled out!

TOM. Tell me. What did you spill? I want to hear what you spilled.

BETH. Look, this is sick. I'm exhausted. Aren't you exhausted, Tom?

TOM. *(Over "Aren't you exhausted, Tom?")* I want to know what was said. Do you mind? I'm entitled to know.

BETH. You *know* all this, we've been through this a dozen times.

TOM. *(Over "... a dozen times.")* If you're gonna be speaking for the both of us, the least you could do ...

BETH. I told them what happened. Okay?

TOM. Everything?

BETH. *(A beat.)* Yes.

TOM. And what did they say?

BETH. They were shocked. They were sad.

TOM. They were?

BETH. What do you think? They're our best friends. Of course, they were shocked, they were terribly upset.

TOM. They were sad for *you*, though, right? Because *I'm* such a bastard.

BETH. They were sad for everybody. They were sad for the kids.

TOM. Did you tell them what you did to me, how you killed my self-confidence?

BETH. Oh, Christ, Tom ...

TOM. *(Continuous.)* Did you? Did you tell them how you refused to hear me? How I tried to get you to listen to me — for years — but you wouldn't? Did you tell them that?

BETH. *(Over "Did you tell them that?")* No more of this. Please?

TOM. I cried out for help, so many times ...

BETH. How did you cry out, Tom, by fucking stewardesses?

TOM. Goddammit, she's not a stewardess!

BETH. Were your cries detectable by *human* ears, Tom, or could just the *dogs* in the neighborhood hear them?

TOM. That's right, go ahead, cut me down, castrate me all over again.

BETH. *(Over "... all over again.")* Oh, please. You know, I hear you say this stuff, Tom ... I can't believe that someone I could have been married to, for *twelve years!*, that I could have had *children* with!, would be capable of spouting such banal bullshit!

25

TOM. Even now! Even now you're doing it! Even now you refuse to hear me!

BETH. I "hear" you, I "hear" you! Christ! Tell me your *girl*friend feeds you this crap, Tommy, I can't believe you came up with it on your own!

TOM. Don't patronize me; I don't need *Nancy* to tell me what I'm feeling …

BETH. *(Over "I don't need Nancy to …")* Don't talk to me about being patronized! You patronized *me,* all along! From the very beginning!

TOM. I patronized *you?*

BETH. Yes! Admit it, you never took me seriously as an artist! Never!

TOM. *(Over "Never!")* Oh, for God's sake …

BETH. You didn't! You never really supported me!

TOM. I supported you! I supported you our entire marriage, how can you say I didn't support you?! You got a great deal! You needed more time to yourself? Help with the kids? I got you a nanny …

BETH. *Me* a nanny?

TOM. *(Continuous.)* You needed your own space? I built you one over the garage! God only knows what the hell you *do* up there all day.

BETH. All I ever wanted from you was *respect,* you know that? For me, for my art …

TOM. Ah, your art, your art.

BETH. What's the use? Get out of here. Go. Get out.

TOM. *(Over "Go …")* You held this marriage *hostage* to your goddamn art!

BETH. Out!

TOM. Do you know what it's like having to support something you don't believe in? Do you, Beth? Do you? It's exhausting.

BETH. *(Turning away.)* I don't want to talk anymore …

TOM. The lying, lying to you, lying to myself …

BETH. Go away! Get out!

TOM. *(Over "Get out!")* What was I supposed to tell you, that I thought your "art" sucked?

BETH. Bastard …

TOM. *(Continuous.)* Huh? Is that what I was supposed to say?

26

That it was just an excuse not to get a fucking job just like everybody else …

BETH. You are such a fucking bastard.

TOM. *(Continuous.)* … and really *do* something with your life?!

BETH. How dare you! How *dare* you!

TOM. *(Continuous.)* I couldn't do that; how could I? Everything depended on perpetuating this myth of talent! *(She strikes him. He grabs her wrists.)* You wanna fight? Huh? You wanna hit me? *(He gets into the bed, straddles her.)*

BETH. *(Overlap.)* Let go of me! Let *go* of me!

TOM. *(Overlap.)* Hit me! Hit me! Go ahead and hit me!

BETH. Prick!

TOM. Bitch! *(She spits in his face. They wrestle, roll around on the bed, inflaming their conflicted passions.)* Ballbreaker!

BETH. Liar!

TOM. Dilettante!

BETH. You fuck!

TOM. Look at me! Look what you've done to me!

BETH. Look what you've done to *me!*

TOM. I could kill you! Right now, I could fucking kill you!

BETH. Try it. I dare you. *(They're looking at one another. He suddenly kisses her hard on the mouth. Pause. Equally aroused, she quickly undoes his pants as lights fade.)*

Scene 3

Gabe and Karen's house. A short time later. Gabe and Karen are on the sofa, finishing off a bottle of wine. Their banter is edgy but always affectionate.

KAREN. Beth and Tom.

GABE. I know.

KAREN. Of all the couples we know ...

GABE. I *know.*

KAREN. Oh, God, Gabe, we introduced them.

GABE. God, you're right. *(They sit in silence, each lost in thought. They shake their heads, sip their wine.)*

KAREN. *(Re: the wine.)* What do you think of the Shiraz?

GABE. Astringent.

KAREN. Uh huh, I think so, too. *(A beat.)* Can you imagine what that would be like? You spend your entire adult life with someone, and it turns out that that person, the one person you completely entrusted your fate to, is an impostor?! Can you *imagine?*

GABE. Now, wait a minute, we don't know the whole story.

KAREN. What is there to know? He was duplicitous; he cheated on her.

GABE. *(Over " ... on her.")* Yeah, yeah, but it can't be as simple as that, Karen, you know that. It never is.

KAREN. That snake.

GABE. Honey. You're talking about someone who up until like two hours ago you thought was salt-of-the-earth!

KAREN. I know; I was wrong. I can't believe I could've been so wrong about a person. Have I ever been so wrong about someone? God, what does this say about my judgment?

GABE. Karen, come on, he's the same person you've known and loved for years.

KAREN. No, he's not; he couldn't be. I'm beginning to think he was never that person.

28

GABE. Honey ...

KAREN. Maybe he never existed at all.

GABE. Come on ...

KAREN. Maybe he was a figment of our collective imagination. He's very seductive, *your* friend. He had us convinced he was true blue. He really did. What a simpatico guy: decent, loving, hard-working, a good father ...

GABE. He *is* all those things. So he made a transgression ...

KAREN. A transgression?!

GABE. *(Continuous.)* It's still the same old Tom ...

KAREN. This is more than a mere transgression! How could I ever look him in the eye again? I can't. After what he's done to Beth and the kids...?

GABE. So, what do we do, abandon him? He's my oldest friend!

KAREN. *(Over "He's my oldest friend!")* I don't expect you to do anything. Do whatever you want. I'm saying, *I* can't look at him anymore.

GABE. Maybe he's really in trouble. Maybe he is. What kind of friends would we be if we went ahead and punished him? I've got a feeling Beth is doing a pretty damn good job punishing him herself.

KAREN. She *is* the injured party ...

GABE. So, what does that mean, she's the injured party, so we can only stay friends with her?

KAREN. I'm telling you I can't *be* friends with him anymore; you can be friends with whomever you like; as far as I'm concerned, someone who conducts his life like this is not to be trusted.

GABE. You are so strict.

KAREN. I am not "strict" — I resent that, that's one of those words ...

GABE. Okay; I'm sorry.

KAREN. *(Continuous.)* I'm principled. You can't fault me for being principled ...

GABE. But doesn't forgiveness enter into it for you, or are you too principled for that?

KAREN. Some things are not forgivable; this is not forgivable.

GABE. Boy ...

KAREN. *(Continuous.)* That's too easy. I'm sorry: Actions have consequences.

GABE. Remind me not to get on your bad side.

KAREN. You do something like this, I'm telling you right now, you are outta here.

GABE. Really?

KAREN. You better believe it. None of that sleeping-in-the-den shit.

GABE. It's for the kids' sake; that's what she said; I can understand that.

KAREN. If he's gonna decimate his family, he doesn't deserve to sleep under the same roof, I'm sorry.

GABE. But it's for the kids!

KAREN. That's a privilege; he's lost that privilege.

GABE. Wow. You are really tough.

KAREN. Don't be facetious! There has got to be a price for doing what he did; this neither/nor situation just won't do. I don't know how she can tolerate that! I would just throw him the hell out.

GABE. So, if in a moment of weakness, I sleep with a check-out girl or something, and am foolish enough to confess to you and beg for your forgiveness, you'd tell me, what, to go fuck myself?

KAREN. That's right.

GABE. You mean we couldn't still be friends?

KAREN. No way. Are you kidding?

GABE. You mean we wouldn't even be civil with one another? *(She shakes her head as if to say, What are you crazy?)* At least now I know where you stand.

KAREN. As if you had any doubt. *(She pulls him closer; he rests his head on her lap.)*

GABE. The thing is, you never know what couples are like when they're alone; you never do. You know *that:* There's no way of knowing. It's all very mysterious.

KAREN. There goes the Vineyard.

GABE. Oh, God, you're right. How would we work that?

KAREN. We couldn't. What, we'd have Beth come with the kids for two weeks, then she would go and Tom would take over? That's ridiculous.

GABE. It sounds awful.

KAREN. What a mess.

GABE. It's like a death, isn't it? *(She nods. Pause.)*

30

KAREN. Why were you so quiet tonight?

GABE. What? What do you mean?

KAREN. When Beth was telling us. You were so silent.

GABE. I wasn't silent. I was shocked, I was stunned.

KAREN. You let me do most of the talking.

GABE. That's not unusual. *(She swats at him.)* Hey! No, I mean it, you *do* do most of the talking.

KAREN. I do not.

GABE. Yes you do. You generally have more to say on any given subject than I do. That's why we work well together: You talk, I write, you edit me.

KAREN. You're evading.

GABE. No, I'm not. Evading what?

KAREN. I think what Beth was telling us ... I think it was very hard for you.

GABE. Of course it was hard. No one wants to hear about his closest friends going through something like this.

KAREN. *(Over "... like this.")* No, no, that's not what I mean. Don't get defensive. It's just, I think, all this ... marital talk ... It's too close to home. I think it made you very uncomfortable.

GABE. Made *me* uncomfortable?

KAREN. Yes.

GABE. Well, like I said, it's not the most pleasant of topics.

KAREN. Don't play dumb with me, Gabe.

GABE. What?!

KAREN. You're playing dumb.

GABE. *(Incensed, he moves away.)* No, I'm not, I don't know what you're talking about.

KAREN. You *do* that, you know, whenever I want you to talk to me about something like this, something important ...

GABE. Oh, great, you trying to pick a fight with me, or what?

KAREN. *(Over "... or what?"; wearily.)* No, Gabe ...

GABE. What do you want me to say? That this whole thing scares the shit out of me?

KAREN. Yes!

GABE. Well, it does. Okay?

KAREN. It does me, too. You think you're safe, on solid ground, then all of a sudden the earth cracks open. *(Headlights appear through the windows; a car pulls into the snowy driveway.)*

GABE. Who the hell is that? *(Peers out.)* Oh, shit, you're not gonna believe this, I think it's Tom.

KAREN. You're kidding.

GABE. It *is* Tom.

KAREN. He's supposed to be in Washington.

GABE. Well, he's not; he just pulled into our driveway.

KAREN. *(Starting to go.)* I don't want to see him; tell him I went to bed.

GABE. Karen, come on, you can't do that.

KAREN. He's not here to see me, anyway, he's here to see you; he's *your* friend.

GABE. That's not true. You *love* Tom.

KAREN. No, I thought I did. *(There's a knock at the door.)*

GABE. Karen. Please? *(Another knock. Childlike.)* Don't leave me alone with him? *(Karen relents. Gabe goes to the door to admit Tom.)* Tom. Hi.

TOM. Hi. I know this is crazy; it's really late and everything.

GABE. That's okay, come in.

TOM. I just had to see you guys. *(Gabe nods, meaningfully; Tom hugs him.)*

GABE. *(Softly.)* I know, I know ...

TOM. Here's *another* fine mess I've gotten myself into ...

GABE. I'll say ...

TOM. *(To Karen.)* Hi. *(He presents himself for a hug, but her body language tells us she's not interested.)* It's okay, Karen, you can hug me, I'm not contagious. *(A beat. She coolly drops her guard and lets him hug her.)* Thanks.

KAREN. I thought Beth said you were in Washington.

TOM. Yeah, I never got there. The weather. *(Karen nods.)*

GABE. Hell of a night to be out on the road.

TOM. Yeah, I was slipping and sliding ... I wasn't gonna just drop in on you like this; I was gonna call you on the way over but I forgot to recharge the phone. Sorry, Karen.

KAREN. Don't apologize to *me* ... *(An awkward moment.)*

GABE. *(To Tom.)* So. Have you had dinner?

TOM. Actually, no. Just a crappy sandwich at the airport.

GABE. Let me fix you a plate. *(Karen shoots him a look.)*

TOM. Oh, no, you don't have to do that ...

GABE. It's no problem. Really.

TOM. It's so late ...

KAREN. Tom's right, it really *is* late ...

GABE. *(To Tom.)* Don't worry about it. I think a light supper would be just fine. *(He goes to prepare a plate.)*

TOM. Thanks. *(A beat; calls.)* Hey, you wouldn't happen to have any of that lemon-almond-polenta cake left, would you?

GABE. As a matter of fact we do.

TOM. Oh, great.

KAREN. She told you about that?

TOM. Yeah, she said it was wonderful.

KAREN. You talk about *cake?*

TOM. Yeah. Why not? We *talk* ... *(A beat. Gabe returns.)*

KAREN. Well, you two can bond. I'm going to bed.

TOM. Karen, wait. *(She stops.)* Look, I know this is awkward ...

KAREN. Not at all.

TOM. It's a lot to digest all at once, I know. You're mad at me, I can tell.

KAREN. No, I'm not.

GABE. Karen ...

TOM. This is just what I wanted to avoid: You've already made up your mind.

GABE. No we haven't ...

KAREN. It's very late and I'm tired.

TOM. I wanted us to tell you together. I knew this would happen. And so did she. It was really vindictive of her, it really was.

KAREN. *(Over " ... it really was.")* I don't feel like getting into this with you right now. You drop in, unannounced ...

GABE. Karen ...

TOM. I said I was sorry about that; my car phone was dead ...

KAREN. Yeah, well, I'm going to bed. *(Turns to go.)*

GABE. *(Surprised by her behavior.)* Honey!

TOM. I didn't want a night to go by without seeing you guys.

KAREN. Good night.

TOM. Hey. Aren't you even willing to hear me out? *(She stops.)* I came here ... I mean, really, Karen, don't you think you owe it to me? Owe it to our friendship? You guys mean too much to

33

me to just ...

GABE. *(Over "You guys ... "; gently.)* He's right.

KAREN. Okay, you made your point, Tom; you drove all the way over here in a snowstorm to lobby for our support. That's very politic of you.

TOM. I'm not lobbying for anything. I just think you've got to hear me out. You can't just go by what Beth says.

KAREN. It's pretty unambiguous, isn't it, Tom?

TOM. No. It's not. I'm not the villain here. *(She laughs scoffingly.)* If you insist on seeing me as the villain ... I could tell you things about *Beth* ...

KAREN. Boy, there's just no end to how low you'll stoop, is there?

GABE. *(Over " ... is there?")* Karen ...

TOM. *(Continuous.)* Things that might give you a little perspective on all this ... Did Beth tell you how she wouldn't touch me anymore?

KAREN. I don't want to hear it.

TOM. *(Continuous.)* Huh? She tell you how she stopped touching me?

KAREN. I don't want to *hear* it!

TOM. But, hey, if you don't want to hear it ... If you want to just be pissed at me, fine ...

KAREN. It's so squalid: a stewardess?!

GABE. Karen ...

TOM. *(Overlap.)* What?! Is that what she told you?!

KAREN. *(Continuous.)* I mean, really, couldn't you do better than that?

TOM. *(Continuous.)* Nancy's not a stewardess, she's a travel agent, okay?

KAREN. *(Over " ... okay?")* I don't care what she is, Tom. The point is you fucked her.

GABE. *(Winces.)* Gosh, Karen ...

TOM. *(To Karen.)* What are you so angry about? *(To Gabe.)* Jesus, she acts as if I ... *(Gabe shrugs.)*

KAREN. Any man who would do that to his wife, to his family ...

TOM. Do you think I'd do something like break up my family lightly? Do you, Karen? Is that what you think of me?

KAREN. I don't know *what* I think of you, Tom. I honestly don't.

GABE. Karen ...

34

KAREN. All I know is, she'd better be worth it.

GABE. *(To Karen.)* Look, maybe you'd *better* go to bed.

KAREN. Maybe I should. *(A beat.)* Good night, boys. *(She goes upstairs. Pause.)*

GABE. Boy, if this is any indication of what it would be like if *I* ever ...

TOM. Man! I knew she wasn't gonna make it easy ...

GABE. Give it some time. This is all very new for us, you know. *(Tom nods. Re: the plate.)* I could throw it in the oven if you like.

TOM. *(Over " ... if you like.")* No no, this is fine, it looks magnificent.

GABE. Wine?

TOM. Please. *(Gabe pours him a glass.)* Thanks. I want you to know, I really appreciate this. I've been feeling so uprooted these days ...

GABE. That's understandable.

TOM. Sleeping in the den, living out of a suitcase ... *(He tastes the lamb.)* Mmm!

GABE. Good?

TOM. Uh! How'd you do it?

GABE. Very simple. You marinate it overnight ...

TOM. Yeah...?

GABE. Lemon juice, olive oil, garlic, rosemary ... Then you throw it on the grill, sear it ...

TOM. Oh, it's fantastic.

GABE. Thanks. *(Gabe watches Tom eat.)* Beth thinks you're having a breakdown.

TOM. Of *course* Beth thinks I'm having a breakdown. If you were Beth, wouldn't *you* prefer to think that? I haven't gone crazy, Gabe, I've gone sane. I feel better now than I have in a long, long time.

GABE. If only you'd confided in me ...

TOM. Gabe ...

GABE. No, really: if only you'd told me what was going on in your head ...

TOM. What, then you'd've tried to "reason" with me?

GABE. Yes.

TOM. Maybe I didn't want to be reasonable. I've been reasonable my whole life ...

GABE. I could've helped you avoid this mess.

35

TOM. See, you see it as a mess and I see it as the best thing that could've happened to me!

GABE. What is it, Tom? Is it just sex?

TOM. *Just* sex? No. It's not *just* sex. Well, of course that's part of it. You know? Ironically? Lately? The sex has been great.

GABE. You mean you and Beth...?

TOM. Uh huh.

GABE. You and Beth are still having sex?

TOM. Yeah. Why?

GABE. I don't know, it seems to me that given the circumstances ... the level of hatred and animosity ... I don't necessarily see how combat is conducive to great sex.

TOM. Oh, God, it's been so intense! If the sex had been this good when we still had a marriage ...

GABE. I must be really out of it. I thought really good sex was the product of trust and love and mutual respect.

TOM. You're kidding, right? Don't underestimate rage; rage can be an amazing aphrodisiac.

GABE. Huh.

TOM. *(Tastes the cake.)* Mmm! It's really polenta!

GABE. Yeah, there's no white flour in it, just polenta. So you're still making love, huh.

TOM. I wouldn't exactly call it making love. *(A beat.)* Beth really wouldn't touch me much anymore.

GABE. What do you mean?

TOM. I mean, the way someone who loved you might casually slip a hand through your arm or onto your shoulder or something. *(A beat.)* I did an experiment. I decided I wasn't going to touch her and see how long it would take before she touched me. I'm not talking about sex now; I'm talking about skin-to-skin contact. A simple good night kiss, holding hands. She wouldn't touch me, Gabe. At all. I gave it a week. I couldn't stand it. I broke down and cried.

GABE. Gee ...

TOM. I don't know about you, but I'm at the point in my life where I want to enjoy myself. I don't want to go through life hoping I'm gonna get lucky with my own *wife*. You know? You go to bed and you think you're gonna have sex and then you say something, some kind of offhanded remark of no consequence whatsoever, and it pisses her off and the mood is gone and it's lights out and that's it. I must've masturbated more than any married man in history.

GABE. I doubt that. Besides, who ever said marriage meant sex twenty-four hours on demand?

TOM. I'm not asking for it twenty-four hours a day, all I'm asking for is a little affection. *(Gabe nods. Pause.)*

GABE. Have there been other women?

TOM. *(Offended.)* No!

GABE. Sorry.

TOM. No, Gabe, there were no other women. There *were* opportunities, though. I mean, when you're out of town as much as *I* am ... You're lonely, you're far from home, it doesn't seem like you're living in real time. I'd be in a hotel bar and strike up a conversation with a female colleague, or some divorcee with big hair, and I'd make them laugh and they'd look pretty and I'd feel competent again, you know?, and think, Gee, maybe I *am* still clever and attractive after all. There'd be that electricity in the air, that kind of buzz I hadn't felt since college, remember?, when a single move, any move at all, and there'd be sex? But I'd get scared and say goodnight and go back to my room and call Beth out of guilt, or hope, and get some shit about something I neglected to do or did badly. Well, by the time I met Nancy — she made me feel good from the first time I talked to her on the phone — I hadn't even laid eyes on her yet — she booked all my travel.

GABE. Uh huh.

TOM. She had this great laugh and this flirty sense of humor, and she said, "We've been talking for weeks, I want to meet you already!" And I began to think, Why the hell not? What am I saving myself for? This hypercritical woman waiting for me back home? Who looks at me with withering disappointment. All the time. This accusatory, how-could-you-be-so-thoughtless look. So, on one hand, there's this *delightful* woman who makes me feel worthwhile and there's this *other* woman, my *wife*, who makes me feel like shit. Who would *you* choose? *(Pause.)*

GABE. So what happens now, Tommy?

TOM. What do you mean what happens now?

GABE. I mean, what are you gonna do? Are you gonna go to

someone?

TOM. *Go* to someone?

GABE. A counselor or a therapist or something?

TOM. What would be the point?

GABE. The point? Tom, we're talking about your family.

TOM. But the marriage is over. What have I been telling you? It's over.

GABE. *(Over "It's over.")* How do you *know* it's over?

TOM. Because I *know*. Because as far as I'm concerned it *is* over, it's been over for me for a long time.

GABE. Yeah, that's how you feel now, in the heat of the moment. But don't you want to be absolutely sure you're making the right decision?

TOM. I *am* making the right decision. Are you questioning my decision?

GABE. Well ...

TOM. *Are* you?

GABE. No. I mean, if I were you ...

TOM. You're not me.

GABE. *(Backing off.)* Okay. *(A beat.)* All I'm saying is, Tommy, if I were you, I would want to be certain that there was absolutely no hope whatsoever.

TOM. *(Annoyed; over " ... whatsoever.")* Oh, man ...

GABE. I mean, how can you walk away, Tom? How can you throw up your hands and walk away? I don't get it.

TOM. Christ, Gabe ...

GABE. Twelve years. Don't you think you owe it to your kids?

TOM. I stuck it out *this* long for my kids. It doesn't make sense anymore; it's not doing anybody any good.

GABE. Yeah, but what if this is a transient thing ...

TOM. Shit ...

GABE. *(Continuous.)* ... or a, a mid-life *crisis*-thing or something? Don't you want to know if it's something that'll pass before you do something irrevocable?

TOM. Look, this is not what I wanted from you, okay? If you were really my friend ...

GABE. Of course I'm your friend, asshole. What do you *mean* if I were really your friend?

TOM. *(Over " … your friend?")* If you were really my friend, you would just listen.

GABE. Just listen?

TOM. Yes.

GABE. Is that what you want? I'm not supposed to say a word?

TOM. I don't *want* your advice; I don't *want* to know what you think, I just want you to hear me. Is that asking too much?

GABE. Jesus, Tom, you drop this bomb on us … We're going to have opinions.

TOM. Yeah, well, I don't want to hear them. All right? My head is spinning with shoulds and shouldn'ts. I've been through all this stuff, over and over. It may be news to *you* but I've been living with this for a long time. I've made up my mind. I just need you to hear me out.

GABE. All right. Talk. Go ahead.

TOM. *(Softly.)* Never mind.

GABE. Talk. I'm all ears. My lips are sealed. *(Throws away the key.)*

TOM. *(Pause; with difficulty.)* I … I hope you never know … the … *loneliness* I've known. I hope you never do. *(He gets up.)* Well … *(He gets his jacket, starts to go.)*

GABE. Hey. Tommy. Don't go. I'll let you talk. I will. I'll keep my mouth shut.

TOM. *(Patting Gabe's arm.)* Thanks for dinner.

GABE. Tom.

TOM. See ya. *(Tom waves and goes. His car pulls away. Gabe turns off the lamps. He sits, deep in thought, in near darkness for a moment. The stairway light comes on.)*

KAREN. *(Off, from the stairs.)* Gabe?

GABE. Yeah?

KAREN. *(Off.)* So? How was that?

GABE. Okay.

KAREN. *(Off.)* Come to bed and tell me.

GABE. In a minute. *(He lingers, looking around the dimly lit room which suddenly feels cold and strange to him.)*

KAREN. *(Off.)* Honey?

GABE. *(Calls.)* Coming. *(He remains seated as the lights fade.)*

End of Act One

39

ACT TWO

Scene 1

In the black, we hear something like the "All Things Considered" theme. Lights Up: A house on a hill on Martha's Vineyard. Twelve and a half years earlier. Much of this utilitarian 1960s-vintage house (which was built by Gabe's family) is made of glass, so the view overlooking the ocean is pretty spectacular. The large main room is used for sitting, dining, and cooking. An exterior deck which wraps around the house is visible through the huge windows. It is around six on a summer evening; daylight fades to dusk during the course of the scene. Karen is preparing a marinade of soy sauce, balsamic vinegar, lime, ginger, and garlic. Gabe enters with bags of groceries, flowers, liquor. Everyone has more hair.

GABE. Hi-i-i.
KAREN. Hi-i-i. Where'd you go?
GABE. I stopped at Morning Glory. I thought we could use some flowers.
KAREN. Nice. *(They kiss. He arranges the flowers in a bottle.)*
GABE. Tom here yet?
KAREN. No, no sign of him.
GABE. Where's your friend Beth?
KAREN. She's still not back from her walk.
GABE. Ah, yes, communing with the skunk population, teaching them *tai' chi* or something. Did you get a load of the relaxation tapes she listens to? She listens to them constantly.
KAREN. *(With mild disapproval.)* Gabe ...
GABE. *(Continuous.)* All that shimmery, tinkly new-age shit.

40

KAREN. So what? It helps her relax. It's not like she's subjecting *you* to it …

GABE. Yes she is; I can hear the treble through her headphones. I don't know how she can listen to that stuff: It would just send me running to the bathroom all the time. What's she so tense about, anyway?

KAREN. Well, she *is* a little high-strung …

GABE. High-strung: great. Hey, *I* know: Let's introduce her to Tom! Tom'll bring her down to earth.

KAREN. She's fun. Besides, I do think Tom could be good for her, he's essentially a good guy waiting-to-happen. He just needs to find the right woman.

GABE. Uh huh. And Beth is the right woman.

KAREN. I don't know; maybe. What's wrong with Beth?

GABE. Have you seen her sketchbook? Whoa.

KAREN. There's no harm in introducing them … What's the worst that could happen? *(He unpacks liquor: four whites, four reds, dark rum, gin, tonic, and two six-packs of beer.)*

GABE. *(Sarcastically.)* You think we've got enough to drink?

KAREN. We're gonna need every last drop. *(Gabe smiles. A beat. He snuggles behind her and kisses her neck. She continues mincing garlic.)* What are you doing?

GABE. *(Kissing her nape.)* Nothing.

KAREN. Gabe. No, really, what are you doing?

GABE. Can't I kiss my bride?

KAREN. Go ahead, kiss your bride, but why is it you always get amorous whenever people are about to arrive any minute?

GABE. No I don't.

KAREN. Yes you do. What is *that* about?

GABE. Forget it. *(He gets out the salad spinner, etc.)*

KAREN. Now you're sulking.

GABE. I'm not sulking.

KAREN. Come on, honey, I'm mincing garlic and you're feeling amorous; tell me: what am I supposed to do about this?

GABE. You *could* try putting down the knife. *(Pause. She acquiesces, puts down the knife, leans against the counter. He kisses her.)* That wasn't so bad now, was it? *(She puts her arms around him. An intimate game ensues, played utterly straight, i.e., no baby talk.)*

41

Uh oh.

KAREN. What.

GABE. You know what time it is?

KAREN. What.

GABE. It's time for me to scare you.

KAREN. *(Playing along.)* Oh, no, please don't.

GABE. I do; it's time.

KAREN. No, Gabe, please?

GABE. Sorry. A man's got to do what a man's got to do.

KAREN. Please, please don't.

GABE. Sorry, Sweetie. It can happen any time now.

KAREN. *(Pleading.)* No …

GABE. Any second.

KAREN. Gabe, please …

GABE. Sorry, kid. That's just the way it is. *(A beat. He says, "Boo!" She jumps.)* Works every time. *(She kisses him. Their kissing progresses. Tom, wearing a knapsack, arrives after a long bike ride. He watches them for a moment. Karen catches his eye and abruptly stops.)* What. *(She indicates with her eyes, he turns.)* Oh. Tom. Hi.

TOM. Carry on, don't mind me, it was just getting good.

KAREN. How long have you been standing there?

TOM. Ten, fifteen minutes.

KAREN. Jerk. *(She kisses Tom's cheek.)*

TOM. Nice to see you, too.

GABE. *(Embracing Tom.)* Welcome. How was the ferry?

TOM. Good. Beautiful. Boy, the ride from Vineyard Haven gets longer every year.

GABE. No, you just get *older* every year.

KAREN. We could've picked you up.

TOM. No, I wanted to ride my bike.

GABE. Beer? Wine?

TOM. Yes!

GABE. Which?

TOM. Beer.

KAREN. How were things in the city?

TOM. Sticky. *(Gabe hands him a bottle.)* Thanks. So, you guys look pretty good; you look like you're on vacation or something.

GABE. Funny how that happens.

42

TOM. So where's this woman you're setting me up with?

KAREN. It's not a set-up. *(To Gabe.)* Did you tell him it was a set-up? *(Gabe shrugs.)* Don't call it a set-up. That sounds so cheap and scheming. We just thought you two might like each other, that's all.

TOM. That's okay with me. I have no problem with cheap and scheming.

GABE. It's not like it's a blind date. You already met her.

KAREN. At our wedding.

TOM. Yeah, so you said; I don't remember.

GABE. Remember, right at the end? The woman dancing all by herself on the dance floor doing that weird Kabuki shit?

KAREN. Gabe!

GABE. What.

TOM. *(Simultaneously; to Gabe.)* You're kidding. *(Gabe shakes his head.)* Her?

KAREN. Now, wait a minute, that really isn't fair. It was a wedding! She had a little buzz on, she was feeling expansive.

TOM. So *that's* the woman in question. I didn't actually meet her, but I did *observe* her, yes.

GABE. Yeah, I think Beth *has* been under observation.

KAREN. You know, this is not funny. Beth is really ... she's really a uniquely gifted person.

TOM. Uh huh. That much seemed clear. *(Gabe cracks up.)*

KAREN. *(To Gabe.)* Stop it!

GABE. I'm only joking. Beth is great. You're gonna love her. And this is not a set-up. *(Tom laughs, Karen shakes her head.)*

TOM. So, is she here yet?

GABE. *(Nods.)* She drove up with us Thursday night.

KAREN. She must've gone to the beach to paint or something.

TOM. She paints?

KAREN. Yeah and she's very good, too.

GABE. *(Equivocally.)* Well ...

KAREN. I like her stuff!

TOM. What does she do?

GABE. She does this, I don't know what you'd call it: these Expressionistic, neo-psychotic ...

KAREN. *(Angered.)* Gabe!

GABE. What?

KAREN. Why are you doing this?!

GABE. What does it matter what I think? Tom can decide for himself if he thinks she's any good.

TOM. Yeah.

KAREN. *(Over "… if he thinks she's … ")* You're being incredibly negative and I wish you would cut it out!

GABE. He asked me what I thought! What difference does it make? Jesus … *(They cook in silence.)*

TOM. *(Sarcastically.)* Gee, it's really generous of you guys to be setting your friends up. I guess you just want us to be as happy as you are, huh? That's really sweet.

KAREN. *(Smiling.)* Screw you. *(Beth comes in looking sunburned and pretty, wearing a shoulder bag bursting with art supplies and headphones around her neck. She ignores Tom, who smiles expectantly.)*

BETH. *(Entering.)* Hello?

KAREN. Hi!

GABE. Hi-i-i.

BETH. I'm not late, am I?

GABE. Not at all.

BETH. I totally lost track of time.

KAREN. Where did you go?

BETH. Oh, it was glorious. The light! On the ocean! I walked all the way down to the beach … Where you took me yesterday?

KAREN. Lucy Vincent Beach?

BETH. Yes!

KAREN. Wow, that's some walk.

BETH. Uh! I love this place!

GABE. I know.

BETH. I am in love.

TOM. This your first time on the Vineyard?

BETH. *(Ignores him; to Karen.)* I walked all along the beach, past those spectacular clay cliffs?

KAREN. Uh huh.

BETH. The light!

GABE. I know.

BETH. I'm telling you, the cliffs glow!

KAREN. They do, don't they.

BETH. They're this brilliant terracotta.

KAREN. Uh huh.

BETH. And these people, these beautiful men and women, were cavorting in the clay ...

GABE. Oh, yeah.

BETH. *(Continuous.)* ... and the light on their bodies ...

TOM. Were they naked?

BETH. *(A beat, looking at him for the first time.)* Excuse me?

TOM. I was just wondering if they were naked.

BETH. Some of them.

GABE. I'm sorry; Beth, this is Tom. Tom ...

TOM. Hi. *(He extends his hand; they shake hands.)*

BETH. I remember you. *(To Karen.)* I *do* remember him.

KAREN. I knew you would.

TOM. Wait wait: I don't think we ever ...

BETH. At the wedding. I talked a lot to the woman you were with. She was a public defender.

TOM. Not anymore. I mean, she's still a public defender, I'm just not with her anymore.

BETH. Oh, that's too bad.

TOM. Not necessarily.

BETH. She seemed great.

TOM. *(Equivocally.)* Uh ...

BETH. As I recall, I talked to her a lot more than you did. Maybe if you paid more attention to her ...

GABE. Moving right along ...

KAREN. Would you like something to drink?

BETH. I would *love* something to drink.

GABE. Beer, wine, red, white...? Rum and tonic?

BETH. Oo, yeah, a rum and tonic; a rum and tonic sounds great.

GABE. You got it. *(Gabe prepares one.)*

TOM. So, is this your first trip to the Vineyard?

BETH. Yeah it is. *(Mostly to Karen.)* And now I see what makes people so fanatical about this place: the terrain!

KAREN. Uh huh.

GABE. That's right.

BETH. *(Continuous.)* This amazing mix of sand and cliffs and rolling hills.

45

KAREN. Uh huh.

BETH. It's magical. Like Scotland or something.

TOM. You've been to Scotland?

BETH. No.

TOM. Me, neither. I've been coming here ... Gabe, how long have I been coming here?

GABE. The first time was the summer between freshman and sophomore year, so that's, what, twelve years.

BETH. Wow, you guys have known each other forever, right?

TOM. Uh huh. Yeah.

GABE. *(Simultaneously.)* First day of freshman orientation.

TOM. Was it the first day?

GABE. The first *hour.* We met on line at breakfast. We amused each other with gross comments about the food.

TOM. That's right! I'd forgotten that.

KAREN. Even then he cracked wise about food.

GABE. Only now I get paid for it.

BETH. All these years. That is really remarkable.

GABE. Or really neurotic, depending on how you look at it.

TOM. *(Taking mock offense.)* Hey!

GABE. No, it is, it's great. Tommy and I had this co-dependent thing going: I'd have these paralyzing crushes and he'd hit on these women before I could ever bring myself to make the first move.

TOM. What? That's a lie.

GABE. I'm exaggerating only slightly.

TOM. That is not true.

GABE. Tommy. Bubbie. Think about it.

TOM. All right: Cathy What'shername, I admit.

GABE. Yeah, and what about the other Kathy. There was Kathy with a K and Cathy with a C.

TOM. Right! The Two Kathys. I forgot about that.

GABE. Two Kathys, two broken hearts.

KAREN. Poor thing.

GABE. And Emily, remember Emily? And Mindy Glazer?

TOM. Okay, okay. See now: *Karen* I could go for, but she wouldn't have me.

GABE. *(Mock alarm.)* Ohhhh ...

TOM. He can't give you what I can give you, Karen. I know; I've seen him naked.

KAREN. I have no complaints.

TOM. Touché.

GABE. *(To Karen.)* Thank you. *(He gives her a kiss.)*

BETH. *(To Tom.)* So I guess I'm supposed to say I've heard so much about you.

TOM. Have you?

BETH. Enough. *What* do you do?

TOM. Oh, I'm just another jaded lawyer, burnt-out at thirty-one but hanging in there for want of anything better to do.

BETH. Uh huh.

TOM. And you?

KAREN. Beth's an artist.

BETH. Karen …

KAREN. A damn good artist.

BETH. No …

TOM. Neat.

BETH. "Neat"?

TOM. *You* know … So: *How* do you know Karen?

BETH and KAREN. Doubleday.

TOM. Oh, right.

BETH. In-house promo: She wrote the copy, I designed it.

KAREN. What a team.

TOM. You still there?

BETH. No, I got out.

KAREN. She left me. *(To Beth.)* It's just not the same without you.

BETH. You'll survive.

KAREN. It's not.

BETH. *(To Tom.)* I'm free-lancing now. Now I'm at Warner.

TOM. Uh huh.

BETH. Mass market paperbacks. Direct-mail to booksellers, that sort of thing.

TOM. *(Seemingly with interest.)* Uh *huh.*

BETH. You "Uh *huh*" as if you think what I do is interesting; it's not. If I'm still doing this five years from now, do me a favor, shoot me.

TOM. *(Making eye contact; seductively.)* Okay; if you insist. *(His gaze unnerves Beth.)*

47

KAREN. Beth is really a terrific artist.

BETH. I wish you would stop saying that.

TOM. What kind of stuff do you do? Expressionistic, neo-psychotic…?

BETH. Excuse me? *(Gabe glares at Tom in disbelief.)*

TOM. I mean … What style? Whatayacallit, realistic…?

BETH. I hate labels.

TOM. Oh, okay.

BETH. Do you know art?

TOM. Not really.

BETH. Then why ask for labels? Why not just take it at face value?

TOM. *(Pointing to her notebook.)* Can I see?

BETH. *(Outraged.)* No!

TOM. Oh. Okay.

BETH. Why should I let you see it?

TOM. I don't know, I just …

BETH. I mean, forgive me: Who *are* you to me, anyway? *(Gabe clears his throat, for effect.)*

TOM. You're right, I'm nobody.

BETH. Sharing one's art … That comes with trust. It's a gift. I never show my art on the first date.

TOM. Oh, is this a date? *(Looking to his hosts.)* I thought this *wasn't* a date.

BETH. *(Goes to Karen for refuge.)* So: What can I do? Give me something to do.

GABE. Here. Make a dressing. *(Gives her a jar, ingredients.)*

BETH. How do you want me to do that?

GABE. *(On second thought.)* Mince a shallot.

BETH. What's a shallot? *(Gabe gives her one.)*

TOM. *(Joins Beth.)* So I actually remember you from their wedding, too.

BETH. What do you remember?

TOM. You dancing. Right toward the end. When you were by yourself.

BETH. *(Embarrassed.)* Oh, God, I can't believe you saw me.

TOM. Sure I saw you; I was watching you. You looked beautiful — I mean, your dancing. It was quite a sight. *(Karen and Gabe exchange looks. A beat.)*

BETH. That was a fun wedding.

KAREN. Was it? I don't even remember. Is that my wine?

BETH. *(Over "Is that my wine?")* Oh, come on, you know it was. You guys really know how to throw a wedding.

TOM. *(To Beth.)* They know all this stuff; they're perfect. *(Beth smiles, nods.)*

KAREN. *(Over "You guys really know ... ")* I really don't; I have very little recollection of it, I was in an altered state most of the time.

GABE. Honey, you were a wreck. *(To the others.)* She made me gather everyone together for the ceremony ten minutes early; remember? She was in a panic.

KAREN. It's true; I was.

BETH. I remember.

GABE. *(Continuous.)* She said to me, "If we're gonna do it, let's do it; I want to do it *now.*"

KAREN. It's true.

GABE. *(Continuous.)* So, what did I do, dutiful husband that I am? I rushed around to everyone and said, "Quick, get over there, Karen wants to do it *now!*" I had to push people away from the hors d'ouevres; my future depended on it.

KAREN. I don't think I got to try a single hors d'ouevre.

GABE. You didn't miss anything.

BETH. So does it *feel* different? Being married?

GABE. *(To Karen.)* What do *you* think?

KAREN. I think it does.

GABE. It feels ... calmer than before. *(To Karen.)* Don't you think?

KAREN. Uh huh; it's true. The social pressure that comes with being single is gone.

GABE. Even when we were living together we felt it. Now that we're married ...

KAREN. What was nebulous and noncommittal is now right out-there, in sharp focus: We're married. We're a married couple.

GABE. It's strangely comforting: There's no way out now, you've gone and done it; may as well relax and enjoy yourself. *(Karen playfully pokes him.)*

BETH. It's like, Okay, now you can get on with your life.

GABE. Exactly.

BETH. That sounds so wonderful. When you're single, you expend so much energy …

TOM. I know.

BETH. *(Continuous.)* You're always looking, always feeling scrutinized. It's exhausting.

TOM. I wouldn't mind getting married one of these days, having kids, the whole bit.

GABE. So do it.

TOM. This single stuff is getting awfully tired.

BETH. Oh, I know. I never thought I'd *be* in this predicament; I thought I'd be married with two kids by now.

KAREN. You're hardly in a predicament.

TOM. *(To Gabe and Karen.)* I mean, I look at you guys and I think, Why not? What am I so scared of anyway?

GABE. I don't know, what *are* you? *(A beat. Beth cuts herself.)*

BETH. Oh, shit …

GABE. What.

BETH. Nothing. *(Sucks on her finger.)*

KAREN. What happened?

GABE. She cut herself, that's all.

TOM. She okay?

BETH. It's nothing. Really.

KAREN. *(Comes closer, sees the blood.)* Beth …

GABE. *(Turns on the water.)* Leave it under the water.

TOM. Have you got any Band-Aids or something?

BETH. It's nothing. God!

GABE. *(Re: the running water.)* Just leave it …

KAREN. *(Overlap.)* Uh, look under there. *(Tom looks. Karen gives a towel to Beth.)* Here. Put pressure on it.

BETH. Would everybody please…? I'm all right. Really. It's just a stupid cut.

KAREN. Are you sure? Let me see.

GABE. It's really not that bad.

KAREN. We just sharpened those knives; I should've warned you.

BETH. It's all right; it's not your fault. Forget about it, I'm fine. *(She holds the cloth against her finger; Tom finds Band-Aids, goes to her.)*

TOM. All right, where's the patient?

KAREN. Over here, Doctor.

TOM. *(To Beth.)* This is gonna hurt *you* a lot more than it's gonna hurt *me. (He sits with her and wraps a Band-Aid on her finger.)*

BETH. Thank you.

GABE. *(Changing the subject.)* Look at that sky!

KAREN. Ooo!

GABE. Come, let's go see. *(Gabe and Karen go out to admire the sunset so that Beth and Tom can be alone.)*

BETH. I'm so embarrassed.

TOM. Don't be.

BETH. I feel like such an idiot.

TOM. Why?

BETH. I was just trying to be a good little houseguest and it's like I end up in the emergency room ...

TOM. Don't worry about it. Gabe and Karen's job is to make the rest of the world feel incompetent; it's their *job. (She laughs. An electric silence. Feeling the attraction, her impulse is to flee.)*

BETH. You, uh, want to go out there?

TOM. Yeah, sure. *(She finishes her drink.)* I'll freshen that up for you.

BETH. *(Smiles.)* Thanks. *(Goes; entering the deck.)* Oh, wow!

KAREN. *(Returning.)* It's such a beautiful night, we've *got* to eat outside. *(She gathers things to bring outside. Tom fixes Beth's drink.)* You've got to see that sky.

TOM. I will ... What's for dinner?

KAREN. Bluefish, corn, salad. Nothing special.

TOM. Sounds great. *(He lightly touches her hair for a beat before she realizes it.)*

KAREN. What.

TOM. You've gotten sun.

KAREN. Oh, I know.

TOM. It looks nice.

KAREN. Thanks. My hair always lightens in the summer. *(Pause. He touches her hair again. She looks at him.)* What are you doing? *(He shrugs, nothing. It's strangely charged for a moment; Karen dispels it. On the move:)* Do me a favor, grab the wine on your way out? *(She and Gabe meet in the doorway. To Gabe.)* Oh, Citronella.

GABE. Got 'em. *(They exchange a kiss as he comes in for some stuff and she goes out. To Tom:)* So, what do you think of Beth?

TOM. *(Equivocally.)* She's nice. She's intense. Better yet, what does she think of me?

GABE. I don't know, I think she likes you.

TOM. Yeah? Then I like her.

GABE. Uh, you're so deep.

BETH. *(From the deck.)* Tom, get out here. You're gonna miss the sunset.

GABE. *(To Tom.)* Go. Destiny calls. *(They join the women on the deck. Responding to the sunset.)* Oh, wow…!

BETH. *(Off.)* Isn't that incredible?

TOM. *(Off.)* It is. It really is.

Scene 2

At rise: Karen and Gabe's garden patio. Present day. Spring. Karen and Beth set the patio table and proceed to have lunch.

BETH. *(Entering, mid-conversation.)* When you promise your little girl you're gonna call at eight o'clock and eight o'clock comes and goes …

KAREN. Oh, no …

BETH. *(Continuous.) And* nine, *and* ten …

KAREN. That's terrible.

BETH. She's devastated — sobbing! — and *I'm* the one who has to do damage control!

KAREN. The poor kid …

BETH. *(Continuous.) He's* out somewhere cavorting with his *girl*-friend, and Laurie's leaving all these heartbreaking messages on his voice mail: "Daddy, where are you, Daddy?"

KAREN. Oh, God …

BETH. *(Continuous.)* He just doesn't get it!

KAREN. Did he finally call?

BETH. Yeah! At one o'clock in the morning!

KAREN. No!

BETH. "Tell Laurie I'm really sorry."

KAREN. What a schmuck.

BETH. "If you want to tell your daughter you're sorry, call her when she's *awake* and tell her yourself!"

KAREN. Unbelievable. Was he always like this or is this what happens to people when they break up? Do they get stupid, or what?

BETH. I know!

KAREN. I'm telling you, this whole thing with you and Tom ... It's like men get by for years without really talking to you and then, one day, when they finally do, it's to tell you they're leaving.

BETH. You and *Gabe* talk ...

KAREN. *(Equivocally.)* Yeah ... *(A beat.)* You sure you don't mind eating outside?

BETH. Not at all; the sun feels great.

KAREN. I feel like I haven't seen you in ages!

BETH. I know.

KAREN. You look wonderful! You really do!

BETH. Thank you.

KAREN. We were worried about you.

BETH. Really?

KAREN. You disappeared on us.

BETH. I didn't mean to.

KAREN. I'd leave messages and you wouldn't call back right away ...

BETH. *(Over " ... right away ... ")* I know, I'm sorry, I needed some time to myself. *You* know.

KAREN. *(Nods, then.)* You're not mad at me or anything, are you.

BETH. *(Over " ... are you?")* Mad at you? Why should I be mad at you?

KAREN. I don't know ... When this thing first happened, we talked all the time.

BETH. I know.

KAREN. You dropped *by* all the time, then after a while ...

BETH. I thought you were getting sick of me.

KAREN. No ...

BETH. *I* was getting sick of me.

53

KAREN. Are you sure I didn't offend you in some way?

BETH. *(Over " … in some way?")* Karen, why would you have offended me?

KAREN. You don't think, on some level, you blame me for this whole thing?

BETH. *(Over "… whole thing?")* Oh, God, that is ridiculous!

KAREN. It was my idea to introduce you.

BETH. So what?! We were grown-ups, we knew what we were doing.

KAREN. Yeah, but I set this whole thing in motion. All the rancor and rage, the pain the kids are going through …

BETH. It was out of your control. That we came together was as much out of your control as our falling apart. You can't control everything, Karen, even though you'd like to think you can. *(Silence.)*

KAREN. So, I guess you immersed yourself in your work all this time, which was probably the healthiest thing you could've done …

BETH. Well, actually, no, I haven't been in my studio in weeks.

KAREN. How come?

BETH. The pressure to paint has totally lifted.

KAREN. Oh, that'll pass …

BETH. Oh, I'm not worried about it; I don't want to paint anymore.

KAREN. Why?

BETH. Right after Tom left … This *unburdening* took place. I looked at what I'd been doing with my life and it seemed so insignificant to me.

KAREN. *(Reassuring.)* No …

BETH. Yes. I realized Tom was right: I *was* using painting as an excuse not to get on with my life.

KAREN. How can you say that? After all these years? All that hard work?

BETH. Let's face it, I was never very good.

KAREN. That's not true, you're *very* good.

BETH. Karen, you don't have to say that anymore.

KAREN. I *like* your stuff.

BETH. It's okay; I'm over it; it's not important anymore.

KAREN. Wow. So what have you been doing with yourself all winter?

BETH. Well, therapy twice a week ...

KAREN. Good ...

BETH. And ... I'm seeing someone.

KAREN. *(A bit taken aback.)* Why, you little devil. Isn't that great!

BETH. It is. He's a wonderful man.

KAREN. What's his name?

BETH. David.

KAREN. Uh huh. How'd you meet him?

BETH. Actually, I met him years ago, like ten years ago or something.

KAREN. Oh, yeah?

BETH. He and Tom used to work together.

KAREN. Uh oh: another lawyer.

BETH. Yeah, right.

KAREN. Oh, well, can't have everything.

BETH. *Any*way, he just happened to call, for Tom ...

KAREN. Uh huh.

BETH. *(Continuous.)* ... and I filled him in on what was going on ...

KAREN. Uh huh.

BETH. *(Continuous.)* ... and he was very compassionate and it turned out *his* marriage was falling apart, too ...

KAREN. Uh huh.

BETH. *(Continuous.)* So we met for a drink and, *you* know, it turned out we had a lot in common. And I've been seeing him ever since.

KAREN. Well, it certainly seems to agree with you.

BETH. Oh, it's been ...

KAREN. I think it's great you're getting your feet wet. The hell with Tom.

BETH. Well, actually, it's a bit more serious than wet feet. *(Karen looks at her intently; Beth giggles.)* I'm sorry. Isn't this silly? This is like high school: I'm blushing. It's been so exciting, stealing away when we can ...

KAREN. How long has this been going on?

BETH. A few months.

KAREN. Uh huh.

BETH. We're having such a good time.

KAREN. A few *months?*

BETH. *(Continuous.)* He's teaching me how to rollerblade!

KAREN. Oh, God.

BETH. I'm getting pretty good at it, too. We play hooky some afternoons and he takes me out to, *you* know, along the canal?

KAREN. Do you wear knee-pads and a helmet and everything?

BETH. Yes.

KAREN. 'Cause you could really hurt yourself on those things.

BETH. It's fun! You should try it. We'll give you and Gabe a lesson.

KAREN. Yeah, I can just see Gabe ...

BETH. He's so full of life: David; he's so open and optimistic. He's a playmate, *that's* what he is, a wonderful playmate.

KAREN. Boy, that was fast.

BETH. What?

KAREN. Tom is barely out the door ...

BETH. Oh, Karen ...

KAREN. You didn't want to be alone for a while? You haven't been alone in a dozen years.

BETH. I've always been alone, don't you see? I spent my *marriage* alone.

KAREN. But to get *involved* with someone, right away?

BETH. *(Over " ... right away?")* I'm in love with him.

KAREN. *(A beat.)* How could you be in love with him?

BETH. I am.

KAREN. *(Continuous.)* You've only just started seeing him.

BETH. I knew him years ago, I said.

KAREN. Through Tom.

BETH. Right. We went out socially a few times, the two couples.

KAREN. But that's different.

BETH. I mean, it's not like he's a stranger. The preliminaries were out of the way. There's a history there. There was already a kind of shorthand.

KAREN. I can understand its being exciting, I can understand that. But love?

BETH. Why is that so hard to believe? I fell in love with Tom that first weekend at the Vineyard.

KAREN. Okay, and look where *that* got you. Sorry. *(A beat.)* I just think you have to be careful.

56

BETH. Karen …

KAREN. *(Continuous.)* You're very vulnerable right now.

BETH. Oh, please …

KAREN. I don't want you to get hurt.

BETH. I'm gonna marry him. *(A tense pause.)* David is not Tom. He's not. They're very different men. There's no hidden agenda with him. What you see is what you get. You know? He *talks* to me; he tells me what he's thinking. He lets me in. *(A beat.)* So much of my marriage to Tom was this dark little tango, this adagio dance. I don't want that anymore. I want another shot at it. With David. And David wants me.

KAREN. *(Nods, then:)* I wish you well.

BETH. Thanks. *(Pause.)* He's great with the kids. You should see him with them. They're crazy about him. Particularly Sammy. He's all over him. Things were so gloomy, after Tom left, you have no idea …

KAREN. I know.

BETH. I never thought my kids would laugh again, I mean it, it was that grim.

KAREN. I'm sure.

BETH. I know what I'm doing, Karen. This is the man I was meant to be with. I really believe that. I had to survive Tom so I could end up with David. It was my fate.

KAREN. That may be, but, still, I wish you'd give it more time.

BETH. And let this moment pass? No way. I don't want to let this moment — look, why do I even bother?

KAREN. What?

BETH. You think I'm crazy.

KAREN. I never said that …

BETH. *(Continuous.)* This is my opportunity for a real marriage, a real partnership. But you don't want me to have that, do you.

KAREN. *(Over " … do you.")* What an outrageous thing to say! Of course I do!

BETH. *(Over " … of course I do!")* I'm finally feeling whole, finally feeling like I'm on the right track, for the first time in my life, and what do you do? You undermine me!

KAREN. I am not undermining you, I'm only thinking of what's best for you.

BETH. Oh; I see.

KAREN. Try being alone for a while. That's what *I* would do …

BETH. *(Over "That's what I would do … ")* What's so great about being alone? Huh? What's so great about it?

KAREN. *(Continuous.)* I would *indulge* myself; get to know myself better …

BETH. That's easy for you to say: You have Gabe, you have this life …

KAREN. Beth …

BETH. You know what I think? I think you *love it* when I'm a mess.

KAREN. What?!

BETH. You do. You love it when I'm all-over-the-place, flailing about. I finally find someone who's like a, like an *anchor* and you don't want to hear about it!

KAREN. That is not true.

BETH. As long as I'm artsy and incompetent, everything is fine. The minute I show any signs of being on an equal footing with you, forget it; you can't deal with it, you have to knock me over!

KAREN. How can you say that?

BETH. Come on, you *need* me to be a mess; you're *invested* in it. Every Karen needs a Beth.

KAREN. That really isn't fair.

BETH. We all play the parts we're handed. I was The Mess, The Ditz, The Comic Relief. You got to be Miss Perfect: everything just right. Just the right wine, just the right spice, just the right husband. How was I supposed to compete with that?

KAREN. Nobody was asking you to compete with anything.

BETH. You're right, there was no contest; I couldn't possibly reciprocate … The hostess gifts you would give me! I could never tell if you were being remedial or just plain hostile.

KAREN. I had no idea you felt this way …

BETH. We can't all be like you, Karen. God knows I've tried. No matter how much *I* stir, my soup still sticks to the pot. *(Pause. In a conciliatory gesture, Beth takes Karen's hand.)*

KAREN. We loved nothing more than having you in our home and cooking you meals.

BETH. We loved it, too.

KAREN. You're my family.

BETH. I know.

KAREN. I spent my first twenty years doing whatever the hell I could do to get *away* from my family and my second twenty years doing everything I could to cobble together a family of my own. I thought if I could *choose* my family this time, if I could make my *friends* my family ...

BETH. Congratulations. The family you've chosen is just as fucked up and fallible as the one you were born into. *(They resume eating in silence.)* How are the boys? *(Karen, distracted, nods.)* And you and Gabe?

KAREN. We're good. We're fine. *(Beth nods. Silence.)*

Scene 3

A bar in Manhattan. Gabe is drinking Pellegrino. He has the self-conscious look of someone drinking alone who is trying not to appear self-conscious; he is waiting for Tom, who is late. He glances at his watch, sips, reads the Times, *looks around, checks his datebook. Tom, looking fit in a smart summer suit, breezes in and joins him.*

TOM. Gabe!

GABE. There you are. *(The men embrace; Tom's hug is more fervent than Gabe's.)*

TOM. Good to see you. God, I miss you.

GABE. Miss you, too.

TOM. Been here long?

GABE. A few minutes.

TOM. Sorry about that. This meeting ...

GABE. *(Shrugs it off, offers a drink.)* Want some?

TOM. Please. *(Gabe fills his glass.)* It's been weeks!

GABE. Months.

TOM. Karen still pissed with me?

GABE. You could say that.

TOM. Boy, she really holds a grudge, doesn't she.

GABE. Well, this is sort of a biggie, though, you gotta admit. *(A beat.)* When'd you get to town?

TOM. This morning. Nancy came *with* me.

GABE. Oh, yeah?

TOM. She loves New York. Thought we'd hang out, see a couple of shows …

GABE. Uh huh. So, you're going up to see the kids?

TOM. No, not this weekend; I have them *next* week. This is *her* week; I'm not gonna mess with *that*, believe me.

GABE. Oh.

TOM. God forbid there's any change of plan … It's like Nuremberg.

GABE. *(A chuckle.)* Uh huh. You look great.

TOM. Thanks, I feel great. I'm running again.

GABE. Oh, yeah?

TOM. I lost a little weight …

GABE. More than a little.

TOM. Nancy and I, we get up at six …

GABE. Wow. Six!

TOM. … run four, five miles …

GABE. How do you do it?

TOM. … come back, make love in the shower …

GABE. Uh huh.

TOM. Then, off to work. That's my new regimen. And let me tell you: It's totally changed my perspective on my day.

GABE. Must be those invigorating showers.

TOM. *(Leaning forward.)* The things she's got me doing, Gabe…!

GABE. Lucky you.

TOM. Nancy has more imagination, more daring, more wisdom … I mean, it just goes to show you how age is totally irrelevant. I'm a boy-toy at forty-three!

GABE. Uh huh.

TOM. She is so at home in her own body. See, I've never known what that was like. A lover teaches you that, it's something you learn together. Beth and I never had that; she was never comfortable in her own body …

GABE. Really? Gee, I always thought …

TOM. *(Continuous.)* So how could I expect her to be comfortable with *mine?* Nancy and I'll be strolling along and she'll put her hand on my ass or something, just like that, without even thinking about it. With Beth, sex was always up to me. It was never about her *wanting* me, it was never about desire, it was all about obligation. And then once the kids came ... Well, *you* know how that is.

GABE. Uh huh.

TOM. Sex became one more thing on my list of things to do. You know? Nancy and I, we are totally in sync. She just has to stroke my *fingers* and I get hard, or give me a look, or laugh a certain way.

GABE. Do you two ever ... talk?

TOM. Oh, yeah. Are you kidding? We talk all the time. Remember what that's like when a relationship is new? All that talk, all that sex, all that laughter? Nancy really hears me. She hears me.

GABE. Uh huh.

TOM. She saved my life, Gabe. She really did; she breathed life back into me.

GABE. *(Nods, then:)* Good. That's great. I'm glad. *(He sips his drink. Tom looks at him.)* What.

TOM. What are you thinking?

GABE. What do you mean?

TOM. Come on, I know *you,* I know that *look* ...

GABE. I'm just listening. You don't want me to say anything, right?

TOM. *(Over " ... right?")* Oh, Christ ...

GABE. No, isn't that what you told me?

TOM. I said that to you ... when I was still very raw ...

GABE. Oh. And you're not so raw anymore? Well, what are the rules, then? You've gotta fill me in here, pal, I've gotta know the rules so I don't step out of bounds.

TOM. Gabe ...

GABE. Okay, you want to know what I'm thinking? I'm thinking: I hear you talking, Tom, I hear these *words* coming out, and you sound like a fucking *moonie* to me, Tom, you really do ...

TOM. *(Over " ... you really do ... ")* I'm trying to tell you ... I was dying! You don't understand that, do you? I was losing the will to live, isn't that dying? The life I was leading had no relationship

61

to who I was or what I wanted. It was deadening. The constant logistics of "You pick up Sam and take him to lollypop tennis, I'll take Laurie to hockey practice ... "

GABE. But, that's ...

TOM. *(Continuous.)* This is what we'd talk about! No, really. This would pass for conversation in our house.

GABE. I know, but ...

TOM. The dog finished me off. Oh, man, that dog. Sarge. It wasn't enough that we had two cats and fish and a guinea pig, no, Beth felt the kids had to have a dog because *she* had a dog. I'd spent my entire adult life cleaning up one form of shit or another, now I was on to *dog* shit. I should've gone into waste management. How do you keep love alive when you're shoveling shit all day long?

GABE. We've all made sacrifices to our kids. It's the price you pay for having a family.

TOM. Yeah, but you have to really want that.

GABE. What do you mean?

TOM. You and Karen: You really wanted it. That's what I realized: I never really did.

GABE. What are you talking about?

TOM. I don't know what I was thinking. It was completely against my nature.

GABE. What was?

TOM. Settling down, having kids. It was just one more thing I did because it was expected of me, not because I had any real passion for it. Like law: It was a foregone conclusion since the age of ten I'd be a lawyer like my father. I always felt, I don't know, *inauthentic* living this life.

GABE. What, you were a party boy trapped in the body of a family man? Tommy, I could swear I actually saw you *enjoy*ing yourself on a number of occasions in the last decade or so.

TOM. Well, sure. But, honestly? Most of the time I was just being a good sport.

GABE. A good sport?!

TOM. You know what I mean ...

GABE. *(Continuous.)* Wait a minute. You were faking it?! You mean to tell me that all those years — all those years, Tom! — the four of us together, raising our kids together, the dinners, the vacations, the hours of videotape, you were just being a good sport?

TOM. No ...

GABE. Then what, Tom, I don't get it. I was there, as well as you. This misery you describe, the agony. Gee, I thought we were all just living our lives, you know? Sharing our humdrum little existences. I *thought* you were there, wholeheartedly there. And now you're saying you had an eye on the clock and a foot out the door?!

TOM. You've got to stop taking this so personally.

GABE. How would *you* take it? You say you were wasting your life, that's what you've said.

TOM. (Over " ... *that's what you've said."*) I don't mean you and Karen. I don't mean *you*, I'd never mean *you*; you're my best friend, I've got to be able to say this stuff to you. I'm talking about my marriage.

GABE. But it's not that simple, Tom. We were there. Karen and Danny and Isaac and I, we were all there, we were all a big part of that terrible life you had to get the hell away from. Isaac's totally freaked out by this, by the way. So when you repudiate your entire adult life ...

TOM. That's not what I've done ...

GABE. That's *essentially* what you've done. And I can understand how you might find it necessary to do that: It must be strangely exhilarating blowing everything to bits.

TOM. Gabe ...

GABE. I mean it. You build something that's precarious in even the best of circumstances and you succeed, or at least you make it *look* like you've succeeded, your *friends* think you have, you had *us* fooled, and then, one day, you blow it all up! It's like, I watch Danny and Isaac sometimes, dump all their toys on the floor, Legos and blocks and train tracks, and build these elaborate cities together. They'll spend hours at it, they'll plan and collaborate, and squabble and negotiate, but they'll do it. And then what do they do? They wreck it! No pause to revel in what they accomplished, no sigh of satisfaction, they just launch into a full-throttle attack, bombs bursting, and tear the whole damn thing apart. *(Pause.)*

TOM. I just want you to be my friend. That's all. I want you to be happy for me.

GABE. Happy for you.

TOM. Happy I turned my life around.

GABE. Sure, Tom. I'm happy for you.

TOM. You know, you can be so fucking smug sometimes.

GABE. What?

TOM. You're not immune to all this, you know. Even you and Karen — *(Stops himself.)*

GABE. What.

TOM. Never mind.

GABE. *What.*

TOM. Come on, Gabe, I've heard you complain.

GABE. Well, sure, we all complain. That's what married friends do: We joke about sex and bellyache about our wives and kids, but that doesn't mean we're about to leave them. Marriages all go through a kind of base-line wretchedness from time to time, but we do what we can to ride those patches out.

TOM. Like *my* parents did? Like *your* parents? They "rode it out" for fifty years! Is that what you'd want me to do? Is it? *(Gabe shakes his head; he doesn't know the answer.)* What kind of example would that be setting for my kids? That we're all powerless to change our lives? You make a mistake? Too bad, you just have to live with it?

GABE. I don't know.

TOM. Don't you ever just want to chuck it all and start all over again? Don't you, Gabe? Come on, admit it.

GABE. Yeah. Sure. Of course I do.

TOM. *(A victory.)* Okay.

GABE. But the feeling passes. The key to civilization, I think, is fighting the impulse to chuck it all. Where would we be with everybody's ids running rampant?

TOM. Look, all I'm saying is, don't do what I did. Don't shut your eyes. I was so steeped in denial and resignation, I know the signs, believe me.

GABE. Why are you doing this? Huh?

TOM. I'm your friend. I'd hate for you to wake up at fifty and …

GABE. You don't get it: I *cling* to Karen; I *cling* to her. Imagining a life without her doesn't excite me, it just makes me anxious.

TOM. *(Backing off.)* Okay …

GABE. It all goes by so fast, Tom, I know. The hair goes, and the

64

waist. And the stamina; the capacity for staying up late, to read or watch a movie, never mind sex. Want to hear a shocker? Karen is pre-menopausal. That's right: My sweetheart, my lover, that sweet girl I lolled around with on endless Sundays, is getting hot flashes. It doesn't seem possible. *(A beat.)* We spend our youth unconscious, feeling immortal, then we marry and have kids and awaken with a shock to mortality, theirs, ours, that's all we see. We worry about them, *their* safety, our *own,* air bags, plane crashes, pederasts, and spend our middle years wanting back the dreamy, carefree part, the part we fucked and pissed away; now we want that back, 'cause now we know how fleeting it all is, now we know, and it just doesn't seem fair that so much is gone when there's really so little left. So, some of us try to regain unconsciousness. Some of us blow up our homes … And others of us … take up piano; I'm taking piano. *(Pause.)*

TOM. *(Mollifyingly.)* Hey …

GABE. *We* had a vow, too, you know, not a marriage but something like it.

TOM. Yeah?

GABE. *(Nods, then.)* We were supposed to get old and fat together, the four of us, and watch each others' kids grow up, and cry together at their weddings …

TOM. It's not like I'm dead, you know …

GABE. *(Looks at him, a beat.)* I guess I mean, I thought we were in this together. You know? For life.

TOM. Isn't that just another way of saying misery loves company? *(Gabe looks at him. A beat.)* I'm kidding. *(Gabe's expression doesn't change.)* Hey, I'll still be there. But it won't be with Beth. *(Gabe nods, but he doesn't agree that Tom will be there. Beat.)* How is she?

GABE. Fine, I think. We actually haven't seen that much of her lately. Karen was supposed to have lunch with her today.

TOM. You meet David yet?

GABE. David?

TOM. *You* know: the guy she's seeing. *(This is news to Gabe, but he hides his surprise.)*

GABE. Oh, yeah, no, we, uh …

TOM. He's actually a very nice guy; I don't hold anything against him. You've got to hand it to him: hanging in there all these years,

65

finally getting what he wanted ...

GABE. Uh huh. How do you mean?

TOM. He really fell for Beth, you know, he was really in love with her. I'm sure she's told you all about it.

GABE. *(Lying.)* Uh huh.

TOM. That's what's so weird about this: We could've broken up back then, when they had their thing, but we stuck it out. Ten years and two kids later, *they're* back together! *(Shakes his head, finishes his drink, looks at the time.)* I'd better go; I told Nancy I'd meet her at Saks. She loves taking me shopping. She hates my ties; she gave me this one for Christmas.

GABE. Nice.

TOM. Listen, I'll call you. Hey, how about, I'm seeing the kids next weekend, what if I ...

GABE. Actually, we're gonna be away next weekend.

TOM. Oh.

GABE. My sister's in New Hampshire. We said we'd ...

TOM. Uh huh. *(Pause.)* Well, next time, then.

GABE. Sure.

TOM. I can't wait for you to meet Nancy. I'm telling you, you're gonna love her. She knows a lot about food.

GABE. Oh, yeah?

TOM. She wants to be a nutritionist.

GABE. Really. I thought she was a travel agent.

TOM. She is. I mean, she doesn't want to do that forever, she wants to go back to school and get a degree, you know.

GABE. Uh huh.

TOM. We'll all go out to dinner, the four of us. How's that? *(Gabe nods; Tom takes out his wallet.)*

GABE. No, no, this is on me.

TOM. You sure? Thanks. I'll get the next one.

GABE. That's right; the next one.

TOM. When's your train? I'll walk out with you.

GABE. Actually, I'm not going home, I'm flying up to the Vineyard.

TOM. Oh, yeah?

GABE. *(Continuous.)* My flight's not till seven. Karen and the boys are driving up right now. We're opening up the house this weekend.

TOM. I can't believe it's already summer.

GABE. Almost.

TOM. I'm jealous. I wish I was going with you.

GABE. Yeah, well … *(A beat.)* Goodbye, Tom. *(They hug for the last time.)*

TOM. I'll call you. *(Gabe nods. Tom starts to go.)* Say hi to Karen if you think she'd be glad to hear from me. And send my love to the boys. Tell Isaac everything's gonna be okay.

GABE. *(Nods, then:)* Bye. *(Tom waves and goes. Gabe's smile fades as he watches him walk away. He smiles and waves again; Tom has looked back one last time.)*

Scene 4

Lights Up: Later that night. Karen and Gabe's bedroom in the house on Martha's Vineyard. Karen is in a nightgown; Gabe is offstage brushing his teeth. He enters in undershirt and boxers. Together, they methodically make their bed before finally getting into it.

KAREN. Are you sure that's what he meant?

GABE. "When they had their thing." What else could that mean?

KAREN. You sure he wasn't just trying to discredit her?

GABE. No no, it wasn't like that; there was nothing malicious about it. He assumed I already knew; that Beth had told us herself.

KAREN. Ten years ago?

GABE. That's what he said.

KAREN. But that wasn't very long after they got married.

GABE. That's right.

KAREN. We saw them practically every weekend in those days, when would she have had time to have an affair?

GABE. I don't know, during the week?

KAREN. That was such a happy time. For all of us.

GABE. I know.

KAREN. There was nothing strange going on, was there? Do you remember any funniness?

GABE. No ... But what do *I* know?

KAREN. I thought it seemed a little too convenient, her white knight surfacing all of a sudden. Why didn't she ever tell me? Who would she have confided in if not me?

GABE. People don't usually go around discussing their affairs, do they? Otherwise they wouldn't be affairs.

KAREN. She could've told me this afternoon.

GABE. How could she? She's spent all these months portraying herself as the wronged woman, she couldn't drop a bombshell like that. Her credibility would've been shot to hell.

KAREN. What does this say about our friendship? What were all those years about? *(Gabe shakes his head.)* So what did you say when he let it slip?

GABE. Nothing.

KAREN. Nothing?! God, Gabe, there you go playing dumb again!

GABE. Why, what would *you* have done?

KAREN. I would've said, "Wait a minute, back up: *What* thing ten years ago?"

GABE. You know what it was? I just didn't have it in me.

KAREN. What do you mean?

GABE. I sat there today, listening to him go on about his new life, and all this great sex, and how wonderful everything is, and, I don't know, I began to feel so sad.

KAREN. *(Sensitively.)* Oh, really, sweetie?

GABE. I felt so detached from him ...

KAREN. Really?

GABE. *(Continuous.)* I could feel myself pulling back, I could see him receding from view, getting smaller and smaller. And I realized ... I don't love him anymore.

KAREN. Oh, honey.

GABE. I don't. Too much was said. I *said* too much, I *learned* too much ...

KAREN. *(Nods, then:)* That's kinda how it felt today with Beth.

GABE. Yeah?

KAREN. Like a whole chunk of our history's been erased and

there's no present tense.

GABE. Uh huh.

KAREN. She's so resentful of me, I had no idea. I don't know how we could ever get back to where we were. Am I judgmental? Am I intolerant?

GABE. Am I supposed to answer that? *(She throws a pillow at him.)*

KAREN. So, how'd you leave it with Tom?

GABE. Oh, you know: the obligatory "We have to get together." He wants us to meet what'shername. Nancy.

KAREN. Oh, God, I couldn't handle it.

GABE. Don't worry, it'll never happen.

KAREN. You really don't think so. *(He shakes his head. They begin to read. Pause.)*

GABE. Remind me in the morning: I promised the boys steamers for dinner tomorrow night. *(She nods. They read in silence.)* He *looks* good ...

KAREN. So does *she*. She's looking pretty again.

GABE. Must be all that incredible sex.

KAREN. Apparently. *(They laugh, then return to their books. Distracted, she puts down her book.)* I had a dream the other night.

GABE. Oh, yeah?

KAREN. We were here, making love; it was so simple and effortless. The way it used to be.

GABE. It still is.

KAREN. Sometimes.

GABE. What is that supposed to mean?

KAREN. Nothing, Gabe; you're missing my point.

GABE. I'm sorry. Go on. *(She shakes her head.)* Please. I want to hear about your dream.

KAREN. *(A beat.)* Remember ... remember how we'd just find ourselves in each other's arms? *(He nods.)* All the time, every time?

GABE. Uh huh.

KAREN. We needed no bridges. That's all I'm saying. It was like that in the dream. We were here, in the dark, and it was delicious, and then I realized, I sensed, in the dream, we weren't alone.

GABE. What do you mean?

KAREN. There were other people in bed with us.

GABE. Uh oh, our parents.

KAREN. No no, not our parents. It was another couple, though, and they were sitting up in bed, alongside us, watching us, analyzing us, whispering in this ongoing commentary, bickering with each other.

GABE. Well, that's easy: Tom and Beth.

KAREN. No, not Tom and Beth.

GABE. No?

KAREN. They were us.

GABE. What do you mean?

KAREN. Both couples were us. Two versions of us, young and middle-aged, in the same bed at the same time.

GABE. Huh. *(He returns to his book. Pause. She's annoyed.)*

KAREN. Is that all you have to say?

GABE. What?

KAREN. Any thoughts?

GABE. Well, uh …

KAREN. *Any*thing?

GABE. I … I really don't know what more to say.

KAREN. Great. Fine.

GABE. No! I mean, you're right, it *is* interesting, the two versions of us co-existing. It *is.*

KAREN. *(Over "It is.")* Never mind.

GABE. Karen …

KAREN. Good night. *(She turns off her lamp, faces away.)*

GABE. Hey. Honey … Honey, come on … *(Pause. He puts down his book and turns off his light. Silence.)*

KAREN. How come the minute the conversation turns to us you're struck mute? Huh, Gabe?

GABE. Uh … I don't know …

KAREN. Why is that? *(He shrugs, shakes his head.)* We can sit here and go on and on about everyone we know and all the problems of the world and the minute I … You know? For a guy who's pretty damn articulate about a number of things … Do you ever wonder about it, Gabe, do you ever wonder why that is?

GABE. Uh, yeah, sometimes …

KAREN. And? *(He shrugs.)* I *tell* you, I *confide* in you this dream I had …

GABE. Uh huh.

70

KAREN. *(Continuous.)* This revealing dream I had about us and you have nothing to say?

GABE. Well, sure I do.

KAREN. What. Speak.

GABE. *(A beat.)* It's ... It obviously ... I think it's about what happens to couples.

KAREN. What.

GABE. I think ... it's the inevitable ... evolution.

KAREN. Inevitable?

GABE. *(Considers this.)* Yes. I think it is.

KAREN. And what is it?

GABE. What.

KAREN. The evolution. Define it.

GABE. You want me to...?

KAREN. Yes! Talk to me, Gabe. Goddamn it, you have got to talk to me!

GABE. Okay. *(A beat.)* It's ... I think it's what happens when ... when practical matters ... begin to outweigh ... abandon. You know?

KAREN. Abandon?

GABE. Uh huh.

KAREN. Is that it? *(Gabe nods.)* Do they have to?

GABE. I think so. *(A beat.)* I *think* so.

KAREN. Why?

GABE. *(Shrugs.)* It's ... I think it's ... *You* know: having kids ... having to pay the mortgage ... making the deadline ... marinating the snapper ...

KAREN. *(Tears in her eyes.)* Don't you ever miss me, Gabe?

GABE. *(Surprised by her sudden emotion.)* What?

KAREN. Don't you ever *miss* me?

GABE. Oh, God, honey, yes. Yes. Sure I miss you. I miss you a lot.

KAREN. *(Almost childlike.)* How do we not get lost? *(Gabe shakes his head. He takes her hand. They're both frightened. Silence. He begins to play their intimate game from long ago.)*

GABE. *(Softly.)* Uh oh.

KAREN. What.

GABE. You know what time it is?

KAREN. What.

71

GABE. It's that time again.

KAREN. *(Catching on.)* Oh, no …

GABE. Yup, I'm afraid so …

KAREN. Not tonight, Gabe, really …

GABE. It's time for me to scare you.

KAREN. Oh, no, Gabe, please don't scare me …

GABE. Sorry, kid, that's just the way it is …

KAREN. Please please don't?

GABE. It can happen any time now …

KAREN. Please, Gabe?

GABE. Any second.

KAREN. No …

GABE. Sorry, kid …

KAREN. No … Please …

GABE. A man's got to do what a man's got to do. *(A beat. Softly.)* Boo! (Startled, she gasps. They hold each other as lights fade.)

End of Play

72

PROPERTY LIST

Dishes
Silverware
Coffee service
Bottle of wine
Wine glasses
Glasses
Bottle of Motrin (KAREN)
Wrapped bundle with place mats (KAREN, TOM)
4 bowls (GABE)
Boy's sneaker (BETH)
Cake with knife (GABE)
Blanket (TOM)
Serving of lamb (GABE)
Knife (KAREN)
Ingredients for marinade (KAREN)
Bag of groceries (GABE) including:
       4 bottles white wine
       4 bottles red wine
       1 bottle dark rum
       1 bottle gin
       1 bottle tonic
       2 six-packs beer
Flowers and empty bottle (GABE)
Salad spinner (GABE)
Shoulder bag with notebook and art supplies (BETH)
Jar and ingredients for salad dressing (GABE)
Shallot (GABE)
Towel (KAREN)
Bottle of Pellegrino (GABE)
New York *Times* (GABE)
Datebook (GABE)
Pillow (KAREN)
2 books (GABE, KAREN)

SOUND EFFECTS

Dog barking
Recorded children's voices
Car pulling into and out of snowy driveway
Ambient bar sounds

AUTHOR'S NOTES

THINGS TO BE CONSIDERED
WHEN STAGING *DINNER WITH FRIENDS*

There are no villains in this play. Gabe and Karen and Tom and Beth are all flawed individuals. It's important that the audience's perceptions and sympathies shift in subtle ways from revelation to revelation. Most importantly, these four people have got to be good company.

The characters must never be allowed to appear ludicrous. Gabe and Karen, for instance, must not be reduced to foodie caricatures. Their interest in food, aside from its being professional, is also aesthetic and sensuous. Resist the impulse to make fun of them; that's too easy.

Don't burden the scenes with too much stuff. Keep the scenery simple and specific. Ideally, a turntable should be used to ensure that transitions are made as seamlessly as possible. I am not a fan of blackouts in which phantom stagehands schlep furniture around.

Don't decide that it should be played as a "yuppie" comedy. That label is both simplistic and inaccurate: These characters are neither young nor urban, and the play is not really a comedy. The key is to be as truthful as possible to the event in each scene. Don't push it. Trust me.

It's important in the first scene that Beth's distraction not come off as disdain for her hosts. They are, after all, very close friends. She is *bemused* by their Karen- and Gabe-ness, not irritated by it.

The Martha's Vineyard flashback scene is the only one in which all four characters appear. There should be an almost improvisational quality to the dialogue and behavior, and it should fly by in a flash. It serves as an animated snapshot of the youthful foursome, containing vivid color and a vitality not found in the contemporary scenes. At the same time, I'd caution you not to overplay their youth (they're not *that* young, they're all in their thirties). And make sure the ironic beats land. We should have an encroaching sense of loss by the scene's end.

The Karen-Beth encounter in the second act is not meant to portray the dissolution of the friendship. They will probably remain friendly but will never again be the intimates they once were. Beth's attack on Karen should be more liberating than deliberately cruel.

The scene between Gabe and Tom that follows *is* a farewell scene. It should not begin as such, but during the course of the exchange it dawns on Gabe (subtextually) that the friendship is irretrievable. Tom's awareness is somewhat more submerged in denial.

The "scaring" game Gabe and Karen play should have a subtle, tonal variation the two times we see it. In the Vineyard scene, it affords us a glimpse of the young lovers' playful sexual abandon; in the end, it conjures that moment but with a combination of ruefulness, hope and fear. The game itself depends on a deadpan quality in order to have the desired effect. And on Gabe's taking his time before delivering the inevitable "Boo!" The final "Boo!" is softer than the first and the flinch it elicits from Karen is smaller still.

Dinner with Friends shouldn't coddle its audience with a pat happy ending. That is not my intention. The embrace that concludes the play is perhaps hopeful but ambiguous. We leave Gabe and Karen clinging to one another in the dark.

Donald Margulies
New Haven, Connecticut
January 2000

NEW PLAYS

★ **CLOSER by Patrick Marber.** Winner of the 1998 Olivier Award for Best Play and the 1999 New York Drama Critics Circle Award for Best Foreign Play. Four lives intertwine over the course of four and a half years in this densely plotted, stinging look at modern love and betrayal. "CLOSER is a sad, savvy, often funny play that casts a steely, unblinking gaze at the world of relationships and lets you come to your own conclusions ... CLOSER does not merely hold your attention; it burrows into you." –*New York Magazine* "A powerful, darkly funny play about the cosmic collision between the sun of love and the comet of desire." –*Newsweek Magazine* [2M, 2W] ISBN: 0-8222-1722-8

★ **THE MOST FABULOUS STORY EVER TOLD by Paul Rudnick.** A stage manager, headset and prompt book at hand, brings the house lights to half, then dark, and cues the creation of the world. Throughout the play, she's in control of everything. In other words, she's either God, or she thinks she is. "Line by line, Mr. Rudnick may be the funniest writer for the stage in the United States today ... One-liners, epigrams, withering put-downs and flashing repartee: These are the candles that Mr. Rudnick lights instead of cursing the darkness ... a testament to the virtues of laughing ... and in laughter, there is something like the memory of Eden." –*The NY Times* "Funny it is ... consistently, rapaciously, deliriously ... easily the funniest play in town." –*Variety* [4M, 5W] ISBN: 0-8222-1720-1

★ **A DOLL'S HOUSE by Henrik Ibsen, adapted by Frank McGuinness.** Winner of the 1997 Tony Award for Best Revival. "New, raw, gut-twisting and gripping. Easily the hottest drama this season." –*USA Today* "Bold, brilliant and alive." –*The Wall Street Journal* "A thunderclap of an evening that takes your breath away." –*Time Magazine* [4M, 4W, 2 boys] ISBN: 0-8222-1636-1

★ **THE HERBAL BED by Peter Whelan.** The play is based on actual events which occurred in Stratford-upon-Avon in the summer of 1613, when William Shakespeare's elder daughter was publicly accused of having a sexual liaison with a married neighbor and family friend. "In his probing new play, THE HERBAL BED ... Peter Whelan muses about a sidelong event in the life of Shakespeare's family and creates a finely textured tapestry of love and lies in the early 17th-century Stratford." –*The NY Times* "It is a first rate drama with interesting moral issues of truth and expediency." –*The NY Post* [5M, 3W] ISBN: 0-8222-1675-2

★ **SNAKEBIT by David Marshall Grant.** A study of modern friendship when put to the test. "... a rather smart and absorbing evening of water-cooler theater, the intimate sort of Off-Broadway experience that has you picking apart the recognizable characters long after the curtain calls." – *The NY Times* "Off-Broadway keeps on presenting us with compelling reasons for going to the theater. The latest is SNAKEBIT, David Marshall Grant's smart new comic drama about being thirtysomething and losing one's way in life." –*The NY Daily News* [3M, 1W] ISBN: 0-8222-1724-4

★ **A QUESTION OF MERCY by David Rabe.** The Obie Award-winning playwright probes the sensitive and controversial issue of doctor-assisted suicide in the age of AIDS in this poignant drama. "There are many devastating ironies in Mr. Rabe's beautifully considered, piercingly clear-eyed work ..." –*The NY Times* "With unsettling candor and disturbing insight, the play arouses pity and understanding of a troubling subject ... Rabe's provocative tale is an affirmation of dignity that rings clear and true." –*Variety* [6M, 1W] ISBN: 0-8222-1643-4

★ **DIMLY PERCEIVED THREATS TO THE SYSTEM by Jon Klein.** Reality and fantasy overlap with hilarious results as this unforgettable family attempts to survive the nineties. "Here's a play whose point about fractured families goes to the heart, mind – and ears." –*The Washington Post* "... an end-of-the-millennium comedy about a family on the verge of a nervous breakdown ... Trenchant and hilarious ..." –*The Baltimore Sun* [2M, 4W] ISBN: 0-8222-1677-9

DRAMATISTS PLAY SERVICE, INC.
440 Park Avenue South, New York, NY 10016 212-683-8960 Fax 212-213-1539
postmaster@dramatists.com www.dramatists.com

NEW PLAYS

★ AS BEES IN HONEY DROWN by Douglas Carter Beane. Winner of the John Gassner Playwriting Award. A hot young novelist finds the subject of his new screenplay in a New York socialite who leads him into the world of *Auntie Mame* and *Breakfast at Tiffany's*, before she takes him for a ride. "A delicious soufflé of a satire … [an] extremely entertaining fable for an age that always chooses image over substance." *–The NY Times* "… A witty assessment of one of the most active and relentless industries in a consumer society … the creation of 'hot' young things, which the media have learned to mass produce with efficiency and zeal." *–The NY Daily News* [3M, 3W, flexible casting] ISBN: 0-8222-1651-5

★ STUPID KIDS by John C. Russell. In rapid, highly stylized scenes, the story follows four high-school students as they make their way from first through eighth period and beyond, struggling with the fears, frustrations, and longings peculiar to youth. "In STUPID KIDS … playwright John C. Russell gets the opera of adolescence to a T … The stylized teenspeak of STUPID KIDS … suggests that Mr. Russell may have hidden a tape recorder under a desk in study hall somewhere and then scoured the tapes for good quotations … it is the kids' insular, ceaselessly churning world, a pre-adult world of Doritos and libidos, that the playwright seeks to lay bare." *–The NY Times* "STUPID KIDS [is] a sharp-edged … whoosh of teen angst and conformity anguish. It is also very funny." *–NY Newsday* [2M, 2W] ISBN: 0-8222-1698-1

★ COLLECTED STORIES by Donald Margulies. From Obie Award-winner Donald Margulies comes a provocative analysis of a student-teacher relationship that turns sour when the protégé becomes a rival. "With his fine ear for detail, Margulies creates an authentic, insular world, and he gives equal weight to the opposing viewpoints of two formidable characters." *–The LA Times* "This is probably Margulies' best play to date …" *–The NY Post* "… always fluid and lively, the play is thick with ideas, like a stock-pot of good stew." *–The Village Voice* [2W] ISBN: 0-8222-1640-X

★ FREEDOMLAND by Amy Freed. An overdue showdown between a son and his father sets off fireworks that illuminate the neurosis, rage and anxiety of one family – and of America at the turn of the millennium. "FREEDOMLAND's more obvious links are to *Buried Child* and *Bosoms and Neglect*. Freed, like Guare, is an inspired wordsmith with a gift for surreal touches in situations grounded in familiar and real territory." *–Curtain Up* [3M, 4W] ISBN: 0-8222-1719-8

★ STOP KISS by Diana Son. A poignant and funny play about the ways, both sudden and slow, that lives can change irrevocably. "There's so much that is vital and exciting about STOP KISS … you want to embrace this young author and cheer her onto other works … the writing on display here is funny and credible … you also will be charmed by its heartfelt characters and up-to-the-minute humor." *–The NY Daily News* "… irresistibly exciting … a sweet, sad, and enchantingly sincere play." *–The NY Times* [3M, 3W] ISBN: 0-8222-1731-7

★ THREE DAYS OF RAIN by Richard Greenberg. The sins of fathers and mothers make for a bittersweet elegy in this poignant and revealing drama. "… a work so perfectly judged it heralds the arrival of a major playwright … Greenberg is extraordinary." *–The NY Daily News* "Greenberg's play is filled with graceful passages that are by turns melancholy, harrowing, and often, quite funny." *–Variety* [2M, 1W] ISBN: 0-8222-1676-0

★ THE WEIR by Conor McPherson. In a bar in rural Ireland, the local men swap spooky stories in an attempt to impress a young woman from Dublin who recently moved into a nearby "haunted" house. However, the tables are soon turned when she spins a yarn of her own. "You shed all sense of time at this beautiful and devious new play." *–The NY Times* "Sheer theatrical magic. I have rarely been so convinced that I have just seen a modern classic. Tremendous." *–The London Daily Telegraph* [4M, 1W] ISBN: 0-8222-1706-6

DRAMATISTS PLAY SERVICE, INC.
440 Park Avenue South, New York, NY 10016 212-683-8960 Fax 212-213-1539
postmaster@dramatists.com www.dramatists.com